Elementary

Christianity

WHAT EVERY BELIEVER NEEDS TO KNOW

HEBREWS 6.1-2

Bob Highlands III

Elementary Christianity
What every believer needs to know.

Copyright © 2015 Robert E. Highlands III

ISBN-13: 978-1502540249

ISBN-10: 150254024X:

BobHighlands.com

Printed in the United States of America

A special thank-you to
April Outlaw for the cover photo.
As my daughter you have always
been the apple of my eye.
As my friend you are cherished and appreciated.
As the mother of my grandchildren you are the best.
May God always richly bless you.
Love Dad

Table of Contents

Elementary Christianity,
what every believer needs to know.

Today was the first day of school for my grandson. He started kindergarten. His mother took a picture of him standing in front of the school and emailed it to the family. He had on his backpack and was carrying his lunch. He had a big smile on his face. He is about to start a learning process that will last for a long time. There is grade school, middle school, high school and most likely college. Yet, what he learns in kindergarten is needed if he is going to be successful the rest of the way. In kindergarten he will learn his ABC's and 123's. Everything will be built on these basic, elementary lessons.

There are elementary teachings every believer needs to know and understand if they are going to grow and mature in their faith. I will tell of my own journey in school in this book and it was not a great start. I did not get the basics and it made everything much harder. Many believers today do not have the basics and it is making their Christian experience difficult and, in some cases, they are losing their way because of it.

This book has one simple goal, to show you the six basic, elementary, foundational truths of the Christian faith. These are clearly stated as the elementary or basics in the book of Hebrews. The writer of Hebrews says he wants to take them beyond the elementary teachings.[1] Then he lists the six elementary teachings as:[2]
1. Repentance from dead works
2. Faith toward God
3. Instructions about washings
4. Laying on of hands
5. The resurrection of the dead
6. Eternal judgment

These are the ABC's and the 123's of the Christian faith. These are the elementary teachings which this book is about.

.

The Foundation

At the beginning of a book there is always the table of content that outlines where the book or study is going. At the beginning of a college class each student is given a syllabus that outlines what the course will cover. This chapter is the introduction to help you understand where we are going and why it is so very important. This set of lessons is about the foundational teachings of the Christian faith.

I remember when I started school. I went to kindergarten in California while my father was in the Army language school. Then he was transferred back to Fort Bragg, NC. I went to first grade there. Then he was transferred to Italy and I went to second grade there. I was such a poor student that when we moved to Germany the next year I had to repeat the second grade. Then we were back in NC for fourth grade. I had been to school in two states and two foreign countries and I was only in the fourth grade. There was a secret I was keeping. I did not know how to read. I had learned my ABC's in kindergarten but I could not read. I had memorized a few words but without the pictures on the page I was totally lost. I had learned to fake my way through school. I was the guy the teachers never called on; they just passed me on to the next teacher the next year. Everything I had learned was by osmosis. I listened and absorbed what I could but, because I could not read, I was always behind and falling further behind every year.

I can remember the day it all changed for me. I was sitting in class at Mary McArthur Elementary School in Fayetteville, NC. I was doing my lessons when suddenly I understood. The thing I needed clicked in my head. Suddenly I discovered that letters made words. That may sound dumb to you, but I did not know before that day that letters turned into words. No one had ever explained that to me. That is a foundational truth you need to learn by first grade but I had not learned it. No one had taught me this basic truth of the English language.

I learned the basic truth needed to begin to read. I was now in fourth grade and I was way behind everyone around me. I slowly started catching up. I was behind in grade school. I was behind in Jr. High. I was behind in High school. I was catching up but I started the reading race over four years after most of the people around me. I was close to being caught up when I arrived in college. I graduated with what would be considered average grades.

Then twenty-nine years later I went back to get my master's degree. I found myself ahead of many of those going to school with me. I was caught up and, since I was older than many of my fellow students I had more experience. When I graduated with my master's degree it was with academic honors. With the right foundation I had caught up and I really enjoyed school for the first time in my life. What a contrast to when, in second grade, I could not read and was held back and in fourth grade when I was the kid the teacher did not call on.

Many Christian believers have no educational foundation to build on. They don't know the basics that everything else is built on. They don't even have the spiritual ABC's they need. They need to learn them so they can start catching up.

Years ago, when I was responsible for our state campgrounds, we were looking to refurbish an old home on the property. It had been built about 90 years before. We found the walls and roof had no insulation. The studs in the walls were boards from two to four feet long nailed together to make eight foot wall supports. There was a bee hive in one wall that was about eight feet across and eight feet high. All of this was nothing. It was when we looked underneath that we found the real surprise. The house had been built on rocks stacked on each other. They were not cemented together; they were just stacked on each other. The whole house was setting on stacks of rocks!

How it had stood for over ninety years was a complete mystery. Two of the stacks of rocks had fallen over. The runners the house was setting on were just boards nailed together on stacks of rock.

The house had to be torn down. It had no foundation at all. It was dangerous, to say the least.

I believe many Christian believers have built their lives on stacks of rocks. They just start piling up some beliefs from here and there and build their whole lives on these and think everything is alright. The problem is, if or when the storm comes or problems arise, they are not ready.

FAKE GREEN BERET

William James Clark[3] loves to pretend he is a Green Beret. He has been doing it for some time now. In 2010 he showed up at a gun show pretending as usual he was a Green Beret. He had the rank of a captain, a Green Beret patch on his arm and was wearing a black beret. Clark lumbered up to an ATV dealer and began trying to get a special deal for "his guys." It did not matter to Clark that he was overweight and out of shape claiming to be a Green Beret on active duty who was wearing a black beret. This is how Clark lived his life. He was all about things like this and it seemed to be just the way he operated. It is not known if he believed his stories or just made them up as he went along.

In 2008 he had called the Russian embassy and told them that his unit was going to assassinate President Vladimir Putin. He felt it was the right thing for a Green Beret unit to do. Hey, what harm could come from some guy pretending to be a Green Beret, even if he only had a black beret.

"On May 26, 2002, the captain of a tugboat lost control of the vessel and collided with the Interstate 40 bridge on the Arkansas River in Oklahoma. What followed was a scene of total chaos -- 14 people died in the disaster. Folks nearby and even the tugboat crew immediately began to render aid to those in the water. You know, like people are wont to do in an emergency. And then fake Green Beret Billy James Clark appeared on the scene.

Clark announced to approximately 20 local, state, and federal responding agencies on the scene that he was in charge. And they believed him. This included staff attached to organizations like the FBI, National Transportation Safety Board, and Army Corps of Engineers. For almost three days, Clark supervised rescue and recovery efforts, which for him meant things like going through the victims' personal effects, commandeering the use of a pickup truck from the local dealership (he told the owner that the National Guard had sent all their vehicles out of the country), and securing seven or eight rooms at a nearby hotel that only he'd use.

Oh, and it turned out that an actual Army officer died in the accident, so "Captain" Clark secured the soldier's briefcase, inside which he found a phone number for the man's widow. Naturally, he took it upon himself to give her the terrible news. You know, as a fellow officer.

Eventually he was called out by the mayor of a nearby small town, and of course Clark turned himself in and apologized for the ruckus caused by assuming command of a situation he was not remotely qualified to handle.

Oh, wait, no! He instead packed up his "borrowed" pickup and headed north to make a run for the border, which he successfully crossed, only to be caught days later and eventually sent to federal prison."[4]

The hurt and harm he did cannot be measured in dollars and cents, but cannot be overstated. William James Clark was a fake, a really bad fake but he was able to fool a lot of people.

FAKE CHRISTIANS

Judas Phygelus is the perfect name for a pretend believer or a fake Christian. Judas[5] was the one who betrayed Jesus and Phygelus[6] was the one who had deserted Paul in Asia when he was needed. They both could be seen as pretenders. When push came to shove they both came up short. The great problem with pretend believers is they, like Captain Clark, work to fool unsuspecting individuals. These pretend believers say some of the dumbest things. They may even believe these things themselves.

- "This too, shall pass." They think Jesus said it on the cross. (it is found in Persian poetry.)
- "Cleanliness is next to godliness." This is the way they explain holiness and righteous living. (it is an ancient proverb - not in the Bible.)
- They think "the little drummer boy" showed up at the manger after the shepherds but before the wise men did. (There is no drummer boy in the story of Jesus.)
- "God helps those who help themselves." This is why they don't give to the church. They are helping themselves. (Ancient Greek Literature. Also Ben Franklin said, "Try first thyself, and after call in God.")
- "To thine own self be true." They think this is from the writings of Saint Paul of Target. (NO, this is from Shakespeare)
- "Love the sinner, hate the sin." This is the foundation of all their religious beliefs. (from writings of St Augustine, and is not in the Bible)
- "God works in mysterious ways." They think this is from Psalms or proverbs. (actually it is from a poem by William Cowper)

If that was not bad enough "A new poll conducted by the Bible Society reveals that more than half of the adults who responded believe "The Hunger Games" are biblical and one in three say "Harry Potter" could be a storyline from the sacred text."[7]

And if you don't get any of these, then this series is made just for you.

But what happens when it is a real emergency and you need someone who knows Jesus. What happens when you need a prayer that reaches heaven? Is this the person you can trust to pray for you? Is this the person who can help you find your spiritual way? I don't think so! Remember the fake Green Beret who took off for Canada when the pressure was on. Where will you find the fake Christian when he or she is really needed?

ELEMENTARY BELIEVER

The writer of Hebrews understood what it took to grow a baby believer into a mature one. He knew there were some basics every believer needed to know. He called these the elementary teachings.

> "Therefore let us leave the ELEMENTARY teachings about Christ and go on to maturity, not laying again the foundation of repentance from acts that lead to death, and of faith in God, instruction about baptisms, the laying on of hands, the resurrection of the dead, and eternal judgment."[8]

The word elementary takes me back to when my kids first started learning. We would hold up two fingers and ask how many. We taught them to write 1, 2, 3... Then came 1+1=2, 1+2=3. This is the basic or elementary level. These six items on the list in the book of Hebrews are the elementary items. They are the 1,2,3... the 1+2=3 of the Christian faith.

I remember helping my youngest son with college math. It was easy at first but then one day we turned the page and it was beyond me. If I ever knew it, well I had forgotten long ago. He had matured in his math skills. This was only possible because he had a foundation to build on.

People want to study Daniel, Ezekiel, and Revelation when they don't know heaven from heartburn or resurrection from judgment. Yes, there is a difference between resurrection and judgment and there are three different heavens in scripture[9]. Resurrection and judgment are separate events in the life of every person, and if you complete these lessons you will understand the difference.

SIX FOUNDATIONAL TRUTHS

The writer of Hebrews said there are six basic or elementary truths of the Christian faith. It does not matter if you are Church of God, Roman Catholic, Baptist, Methodist, or Independent. This is what the Bible says are the elementary or foundational truths we build on. This is where we put our cornerstone, Christ Jesus. These are the syllabus of the faith. Every believer should know them and be able to explain how they are important to them.

1. REPENTANCE from dead works: We need to start from where we are.
2. FAITH toward God: We need to know we cannot do this by ourselves.
3. WASHINGS: We need to be willing to sign on the line.
4. LAYING ON OF HANDS: We need to accept our position.
5. RESURRECTION: We need to know what will happen.
6. JUDGMENT: We need to be ready to face GOD!

These six are what will be covered in the next six lessons. Their importance cannot be overstated. Each one will be laid out in detail.

THE RIGHT FOUNDATION

Jesus understood the importance of the right foundation. He told a parable to illustrate this very point.

"Therefore everyone who hears these words of mine and puts them into practice is like a wise man who built his house on the rock. The rain came down, the streams rose, and the winds blew and beat against that house; yet it did not fall, because it had its foundation on the rock.

But everyone who hears these words of mine and does not put them into practice is like a foolish man who built his house on sand. The rain came down, the streams rose, and the winds blew and beat against that house, and it fell with a great crash."[10]

It takes just as much work to build on a bad foundation as it does to build on a good foundation. The difference is what happens when the foundation is tested. The believer needs the right foundation.

There are some facts about foundations everyone needs to know.

- The foundation always comes first. When you pass a new housing area you can always tell where they are going to build because the foundation is put down first.
- Without the foundation it is only a barn. It has nothing to stand on. It's where you put animals. Faith without a foundation is ripe for all sorts of perversions.
- A bad foundation is only a storm away from collapse. The lives of believers without a solid foundation often end the same way. The first problem that comes their way, they get upset with God and are gone.
- A foundation limits the person. A good foundation allows the person to build a solid building and a

solid faith life. A foundation of stacked rocks will not take the pressure of time.

- A foundation is supposed to last. When they uncover ancient cities they find the foundation of houses. Recently in Jerusalem they started digging under a series of houses and found that they were built on the foundation of three other houses. I have seen houses completely destroyed, and the foundation was all that was left. They just built a new house on the old foundation. This is how some people make it through difficult times, and others don't. We need a foundation that, no matter what happens, we can build on it. This past year, after a tornado in Oklahoma, a woman was interviewed who had lost everything. She was standing in the middle of the foundation of her house holding her baby with her dog at her side. When asked what she would do, she looked down and said 'I have a great foundation to build on so I will start over right here.'
- A foundation needs to be built on solid ground. We do not stand on ourselves; we stand on the truth that is Jesus. He is the solid rock and without him we are the sinking sand.

SIX FOUNDATIONAL TRUTHS

This simple list is foundational to the life of every believer. It starts at salvation, when we repent, and continues until we stand before Jesus to receive our just rewards. In between is our entire life as believers.

1. REPENTANCE: Life's DIRECTION determines where we finish.
2. FAITH: We must have complete CONFIDENCE in God.
3. WASHINGS: Until we learn OBEDIENCE we will never succeed.
4. LAYING ON OF HANDS: Every believer has kingdom RESPONSIBILITIES

5. RESURRECTION : Life on earth will be FINISHED when we die. It is guaranteed: no matter how long you live you will die. That goes for the world's oldest person. "The world's oldest person... died in Japan, aged 116 -- just days after the passing of a Chinese woman with a rival claim to the title."[11] When he passed away, a 115 year old living in Osaka, Japan became the oldest living person. She will not hold the title long because she has an appointment with the resurrection.[12]

6. JUDGMENT: The REWARDS may be positive or negative; you choose. God merely honors the choices we make in life.

So it is time to begin this foundation check. It is time to make sure you know and understand the elementary teachings and truths of the Christian belief system. It is time to start the journey.

Life's Direction

This is the first of six foundational truths every believer needs to know, understand, and apply to their life. This is about your spiritual life journey and if you are going to start this spiritual life journey you need to start at the beginning. Each of these steps is also covered in the first book I wrote about this same subject.[13]

There are words and phrases we hear and they instantly invoke in us an emotion or a feeling. Some of them are mom, dad, love, and chocolate. The first three make sense to everyone. Each word will mean something different to someone. Chocolate is a word that people respond to with emotions. Some people love it, crave it, need it, want it all the time. I am one of those people. I love chocolate, but I cannot have chocolate. It will give me a migraine, and the darker the chocolate the quicker and more intense the migraine will be. So the emotions I feel about the word "chocolate" is a deep desire and a strong hate all at the same time. Now, if you have never considered the amount of chocolate in our world, then the next time you are standing in line at the grocery store just look around. Right at the check stand chocolate is everywhere. There are shelves of chocolate within reach of every man, woman and child. It has been placed there because those who sell it know how bad you want it. It goes all the way to the floor so even the smallest child can see it is there. For the small child it is literally inches from their face. Last week was Valentine's Day and if you want to see chocolate everywhere, that is the season. I went into a bank and there on the counter in front of me were tiny cups filled with chocolate to munch on while you wait. REALLY! Seriously! I had to be strong in the bank and this time it was FREE chocolate. I have to make this choice all the time. Eat chocolate and enjoy the taste I crave, knowing within 24 hours I will be in pain and have to take medicine, or skip chocolate and the great, fabulous taste and also skip the headache. 99% of the time I skip the chocolate, the other 1% I am working on. By the way, I did skip it at the bank even though it was free. I thought about it but I knew if I ate the seven or eight pieces of chocolate incased in a melt in your mouth candy shell I would want to run out and buy a ten pound bag to eat as I drove around on the errands. Then I would have to take two tablets the next day to deal with the migraine. The migraine and trying to explain it to my wife were enough to make me skip the chocolate.

What about religious words that invoke feelings and emotions. There is a religious 'R' word that invokes images in many a red faced preacher with the veins in his neck about to explode. He is pointing his finger at them and he says the 'R' word. To them the 'R' word is about giving up a very happy life and living a life of misery. To them the results of responding to the 'R' word would be equivalent to having to give up chocolate for life, times ten. The 'R' word makes them cringe and hope that their pastor never brings it up while they are attending church.

More on the 'R' word shortly, but right now a parable by Jesus will set the stage for us to understand the "R" word and how to choose life's direction.

CHOOSING LIFE'S DIRECTION

"Jesus told... this story: "A man had two sons. The younger son told his father, 'I want my share of your estate now before you die.' So his father agreed to divide his wealth between his sons.

"A few days later this younger son packed all his belongings and moved to a distant land, and there he wasted all his money in wild living. About the time his money ran out, a great famine swept over the land, and he began to starve. He persuaded a local farmer to hire him, and the man sent him into his fields to feed the pigs. The young man became so hungry that even the pods he was feeding the pigs looked good to him. But no one gave him anything.

"When he finally came to his senses, he said to himself, 'At home even the hired servants have food enough to spare, and here I am dying of hunger! I will go home to my father and say, "Father, I have sinned against both heaven and you, and I am no longer worthy of being called your son. Please take me on as a hired servant."'

"So he returned home to his father. And while he was still a long way off, his father saw him coming. Filled with love and compassion, he ran to his son, embraced him, and kissed him. His son said to him, 'Father, I have sinned against both heaven and you, and I am no longer worthy of being called your son.'*

"But his father said to the servants, 'Quick! Bring the finest robe in the house and put it on him. Get a ring for his finger and sandals for his feet. And kill the calf we have been fattening. We must celebrate with a feast, for this son of mine was dead and has now returned to life. He was lost, but now he is found.' So the party began."[14]

LIFE'S DIRECTIONS

There are really only two directions in life. They both deal with the Father and both have eternal consequences. The first direction we can choose is away from the Father. It is this first one we see the son choose. This first direction away from the father is a trap set by the Devil himself. It is simple and always the same. It is designed to appear to be all happiness and fun. The son was able to "*squander his wealth in wild living*," believing he was enjoying life. It is like when a person takes the first smoke of a cigarette, it is about being in charge. The first use of drugs is about the pleasure and excitement. Every addicted person believed they could quit anytime they wanted to. They did not know about the beast and how he digs into the soul and takes control of the body when they try their first cigarette or hit on a joint. It is designed by the enemy of our soul to bring the person down and to make him fail. In the end the son found that "*no one gave him anything*."

My wife and I stopped at my favorite BBQ place where I ordered the best brisket burger in the world. It is a diet killer and I am glad the restaurant is out of town. My wife was sitting across from me. In the background I could see a TV with sports on. I would glance up occasionally to see what was happening. It was basketball so I was not interested. Then I looked up and there was a young girl's face followed by pictures of her playing sports. Her hairstyle was right out of the 80's. The screen went to black and it read 1989 then it changed over to the word NOW. Then she was back, sitting in a wheelchair. She had a breathing tube inserted into her neck just above her collar. She was pail, thin, and looked sick. Then something about smoking came up on the screen. She had started when she was young and thought she could control it, but she had learned differently. She could not go back; she had lost to the beast. The enemy had won another round. When the son was reduced to feeding the pigs and living in hunger, the enemy thought he had won. Then the son took a personal U-Turn.

The trip away from the Heavenly Father is almost always the same. It is a search for excitement and freedom. It is a journey that takes the person to a point of complete loss, but it is not the loss of money, it is the loss of the soul. It is the loss of the relationship with the father. The son had chosen to leave his father and it was the son who would pay the price.

The second direction a person can choose will take the individual toward the Father. This moves the individual from starving to where there is food to spare. Yet, what does it take to make this transition and why do so few make it? The first thing the son had to do was admit where he was. When he evaluated his life, he said, "*I am starving.*" The alcoholic cannot get help until he admits where he is and that he needs help. Until he says, " I am an alcoholic," he will not seek help.

Then the son said, "*I will go back.*" You have to decide where you want to be. It is not enough to know you have come up short, you need a goal. Each person has to want to live their life for God and with God if they are going to make the decisions needed to find their way back to the Father. Sometime I think preachers want people to believe God is just waiting to beg us to come back to Him. There are many people who know they are not right with God and yet they do nothing about it. They even seem to want to stay as far away from God as they can.

We have to be willing to be honest with God. The son said, "*I have sinned.*" His admission that it was his fault is a key to his change of direction and his acceptance by the father. This world of blame is driving me crazy. There was the 16-Year-Old rich kid's whose defense for drinking, driving and killing four individuals was "Affluenza."[15] He blamed his crime on his parent's money. So, a kid on drugs, who steals liquor from a store and drives around high and drunk, and then at 70 mph plows into another vehicle and kills four, can go to rehab because his parents were too rich to discipline him, is not responsible for his actions. His parents neglected to discipline him and now a judge has chosen to do the same. The boy has been sent to a country club type rehab center. Until you are honest with God you will not get the help you need.

When the son approached the father it was humbly. He was not returning to his father demanding anything. He came to his father and said, "*I am no longer worthy.*" Life direction toward the heavenly father requires our willingness to come to Him and accept what He has for us.

The son had decided to go away from the father. The "*son got together all he had, set off for a distant country.*" He also decided to go back to the father. "*So he got up and went back to his father.*" Each person chooses their life direction either toward the world and away from the Father or toward the Father and away from the world.

In the end it all comes down to the choice of the individual. It comes down to your personal choice of direction, away from the Father or toward the Father.

THE "R" WORD

John the Baptist is often seen as a harsh preacher. He was definitely different. *"John's clothes were made of camel's hair, and he had a leather belt around his waist. His food was locusts and wild honey."*[16] Yet, John was someone the people wanted to be with. They wanted to hear him. *"People went out to him from Jerusalem and all Judea and the whole region of the Jordan*[17]*."* John was preaching a message that included the "R" word and people were flocking to him. John stood in the Jordan River preaching *"Repent, for the Kingdom of heaven is near"*[18]

When Jesus started his ministry he preached, *"Repent, for the kingdom of heaven is near."*[19] Just as they did with John, people streamed out to hear and respond to Jesus. The message to repent was a positive call on their lives.

After the death, resurrection and ascension of Jesus into heaven it was left up to his disciples to give the world his message. After telling people about Jesus and how they were responsible for what had happened to him they ask Peter what they should do. His response was clear. *"Repent and be baptized, every one of you, in the name of Jesus Christ for the forgiveness of your sins."*[20] Did they run away? Did they refuse to listen to him? No, they responded to his message and *"about three thousand were added to their number that day."*[21]

People in Jesus' time responded to the "R" word in a positive way. If we want to understand what it means to "REPENT" we can learn it from Peter and we can see how to apply this to our life. In his second sermon Peter preached to the people, *"Repent, then, and turn to God, so that your sins may be wiped out, that times of refreshing may come from the Lord, and that he may send the Christ, who has been appointed for you—even Jesus."*[22]

There were four simple steps that Peter gave to the people that day as he preached.

1. Peter's call to REPENT meant the people had to "*turn to God*." This is about a change of direction. It is about a personal choice. God does not force the person to repent or change direction He is waiting for the person who does.

2. Peter said if the person REPENTS their "*sins may be wiped out*." This is about the power of what can happen if the person does repent. SIN is not what I say it is and not what you say it is. It is not something we vote on or something that changes depending on who you are. Sin is what God says it is and how He has led the writers of the Bible to say it is. It is something you need to understand before you come to the last of these six steps and stand in judgment before the living God Himself. We will look at the New Testament list when we talk about judgment. I want to give you the broadest definition I know. Sin is when we walk away from God and live our lives as we want. Sin is what the son did to his father. He went away and lived a life of sin. His life centered on what would make him happy at the moment without regard of what the results would be.
Now consider what you are GIVING UP when you turn to God. You give up the stink of sin, the spiritual hunger, the separation from God, the coming eternal sorrow and suffering. Who would not want that? Well, apparently a lot of people.

3. Peter said when the person REPENTS "*times of refreshing may come*." Refreshing is referring to the restoring of life. It is about what the Father wants to do for you. It is being freed from the results of sin.
I need to share a story with you here. When we lived in Southwestern Kansas we would drive to the big city to do our grocery shopping. That meant we would drive an hour to Dodge City to shop. On the way we had to drive past a pig farm. This was a row of low buildings located right beside the road. You

never got to see the pigs. They were in the buildings. These buildings were about a city block long and there was a bunch of them. They were located on a corner of two roads. It did not matter which road we took to Dodge City, we had to pass by that corner. You knew the pig farm was close because you could smell it. We would roll up the windows, close the vents and drive past it as quickly as possible; all the while everyone in the car was holding their breath. Me, my wife and our daughter April were able to hold our breath longer than Shelly Winters did in the Poseidon Adventure. Finally we would be past the pig farm and we would roll down the window, turn on the fan and air out the car. That would take several minutes. It did not matter if it was 100 degrees or 10 degrees, we had to air out the car. Here is my point, PIGS STINK! They stink bad! They stink so bad you can taste it. They stink so bad you want to throw up. Now, think about it, the son had been feeding and living with pigs and he had to stink. He had to stink bad just like pigs. He really needed refreshing.

4. A person repents so "*CHRIST JESUS may be SENT to you.*" If you want Jesus to be part of your life you need to change the direction of your life. WARNING: You do not cleanup for God; God will clean you up. The son returned home in clothes stinking of pigs and sin. It did not matter how far he had to go, they would still smell like pigs. The Father put the clean robe on the son. That meant he had to be cleaned up and everything that had the stink of pigs had to be removed. If you wait till you get the stink of sin off of you before coming to the father for help, you will never get back to the father. The stink of sin is 100 times worse than the stink of pigs. You can never wash it off yourself. The old hymn asks the question, "What can wash away my sins?" and it answers "Nothing but the blood of Jesus." I want you to know that nothing but the blood of Jesus can remove the stink of sin.

UNDERSTANDING SPIRITUAL U-TURNS

The direction of life is in your hands, if you are going the WRONG way. REPENT! You make the decision and have to actually follow through. U-Turns are the place we START! Many times people think if they have repented that is all they need to do. If the son had only looked toward home and thought about how good it was at home but never walked home, that is not repenting. That is regretting where you are, but it is not a change of direction back to the father. Finally, this is about a JOURNEY not an EVENT!

Imagine a couple getting married and after the ceremony the groom looks at the bride and says. "Hey, that was fun, I will always remember this time together here today. I will see you around, hope everything goes well for you. Man I am glad we got married." Then he walks out leaving her there and lives his life just like before he got married.

Well, he got married, that is the event, but marriage is about the journey, the life together. The ceremony is the start of the time together, not just an event they share together and then go their separate ways. The purpose of getting married is a life together. So, marriage is about the journey and is not just an event.

Here is where many misunderstand Christianity. When it comes to the spiritual U-Turn, it is the event, the start of the journey. It is supposed to be the beginning of a person's life with Jesus. This is the start of their life together with Jesus. Yet, many say thanks for forgiving me, for removing the stink and stain of sin. See you around, I will pray and let you know when I need something but I will be going back to my old life. They think the U-Turn is an event and have no plans for the journey.

U-TURN

Remember the four points from what Peter said to them in the first century. Let's just talk about this U-Turn.

When you make a spiritual U-TURN toward God it is an OPPORTUNITY. I am not pointing at you with the veins on my neck bulging, red faced, screaming REPENT! What I am doing is offering you the OPPORTUNITY to make a spiritual U-Turn and begin a life journey with God. This is what it means to repent from dead works. It is leaving the pig farm and heading back to God. It is what John the Baptist, Jesus and Peter were offering.

The results are your SINS will be WIPED out, they are completely GONE. What can wash away your sins? The answer is nothing but the blood of Jesus.

It is what God does for you and not what you can do for yourself. You may choose to return to God but it is God who causes the TIMES of REFRESHING to come. God REMOVES the STINK of sin. When he is done you smell sweet.

You have to repent, make a U-Turn if CHRIST JESUS is going to be SENT to you. This is about discovering the NEW life that comes with a U-Turn. This is not an event but the beginning of a lifelong journey.

"Nothing But the Blood" was written by Robert Wadsworth Lowry in 1876. The words of this poem are a powerful reminder of all Jesus has done for those who are willing to make a U-Turn.

> What can wash away my sin?
> Nothing but the blood of Jesus;
> What can make me whole again?
> Nothing but the blood of Jesus.
>
> For my pardon this I see -
> Nothing but the blood of Jesus;

For my cleansing, this my plea -
Nothing but the blood of Jesus.

Nothing can for sin atone -
Nothing but the blood of Jesus;
Naught of good that I have done -
Nothing but the blood of Jesus.

This is all my hope and peace -
Nothing but the blood of Jesus;
This is all my righteousness -
Nothing but the blood of Jesus.

Oh! precious is the flow
That makes me white as snow;
No other fount I know,
Nothing but the blood of Jesus.

Is it time for you to make a U-Turn? If it is, then REPENT and discover the great opportunity and journey God has laid out for you.

Traveling With God

When a person becomes a follower of Jesus it is no small matter. The new believer has just hooked up with God Almighty, the creator of everything, everywhere, seen and unseen. This is not just a brief meeting when the person gets saved but it is a life long journey they will share together. It is not easy to understand but God has been planning for each person's journey long before they were even born. The only question is whether they are going to pick up their tickets or not, and make the trip with God.

Everyone is on a trip; it is either toward or away from God. The trip toward the Heavenly Father is not one we make alone and it is one we have to make believing He has plans for our lives and everything that is happening will be used of Him. Notice, I did not say anything about how great the journey with Him was going to be. I did not say you always get to go first class. If you want to hear someone lie to you about the journey you can turn on a host of television or internet preachers and they will tell you how God wants you to be rich, never get sick and always be happy, and oh yes, they will ask you to "please send cash."

I want to be careful here, this has been going on for as long as there have been preachers even in the case of the Old Testament prophets. Ahab, the King of Israel and Jehoshaphat King of Judah were in a bind. They did not know whether they should go to war against Ramoth-gilead[23] so they called the prophets together to find out what God wanted them to do. Over 400 prophets were called together to speak for God. They all told the kings to go and fight because God was for them. The prophets assured victory. There was one prophet who was not there. His name was Micaiah. The kings summoned him to come and tell them if he had heard the same thing from God. When Micaiah showed up he found himself standing by himself with the other prophets looking at him. When he was asked what to do, he told the king, "Hey, it is a cinch; your enemies will fall into your hands. Go for it, God is good and God is with you." The tone in his voice must have given him away because the king grew angry and said he did not want a yes man but only the truth. That is when Micaiah changed his tune and his tone. Micaiah then said, "*I saw all Israel scattered on the mountains, Like sheep which have no shepherd; And the LORD said, 'These have no master. Let each of them return to his house in peace.'*"24 In other words, hey king your goose is cooked and someone else is going to eat it and you will not be around to even see it.

The king was furious. He screamed at Micaiah and told him this is exactly what he expected. Then a prophet fight broke out. One of them even hit Micaiah across the face. Here is Micaiah the only one in the room who is not standing and telling the king what he wants to hear. He is speaking truth but it is not the popular message of the day. What is his reward? He is sent back to his home town where he is to be thrown into prison and given nothing but small amounts of bread and water. Micaiah has some parting words for the king. "*If you indeed return safely, the LORD has not spoken by me.*"25 Otherwise, 'Hey if I see you again then I don't speak for God, but I don't expect to ever see you again.' King Ahab took the advice of the 400 plus and ended up dead. Micaiah went back to his small town ministry and became just another prophet, another prophet of truth.

Micaiah was just a nobody from nowhere who was not popular or even well known. He did not jump on the bandwagon to preach what was popular. The key is he was preaching truth and that is all that mattered to him.

You have a choice. You can go out and get the latest book from the big television preacher or internet blogger about how your journey with God is going to be fabulous or you can listen to me. I promise, everything I say is not what you want to hear but everything I say today will be true and it will help you succeed in your life as a believer. Now let's look at the lives of two men and one woman and see what they can teach us about the second truth we need to know as a foundational truth, "FAITH TOWARD GOD."

JOSEPH'S LIFE JOURNEY[26]

- He is born the 11th son of Jacob and Rachel.
- His father Jacob gives him a coat of many colors when he is 17, showing he is the favorite son.
- His brothers become angry, beat him up, and throw in a pit.
- They make it look like he has been killed by a wild animal to fool their father.
- Then they sell him as a slave to some strangers headed toward Egypt.
- He winds up on the auction blocks in Egypt and is sold to a man named Potiphar.
- He serves Potiphar and is put in charge of his whole household for about 10 years; he is about 27 years old.
- Potiphar's wife tries to seduce him and when he refuses she accuses him of trying to rape her.
- He is thrown into prison and is there for about 3 years; He is now 30 years old.
- At age 30, after interpreting some dreams, he is called on by the King to help save Egypt from a coming disaster.
- He is 2nd in command to Pharaoh and running Egypt during very tough times.
- When he is 37 his brothers show up to buy food because the famine has reached them in Israel.
- After a period of time he reveals himself to them and the family is reconciled.
- When he is 39 his family moves to Egypt, this includes his father Jacob, his mother is dead.
- When he is 56 his father Jacob dies
- He lives long enough to see his children, his grand-children, great-grand-children and great, great-grand-children.
- When he is 110, Joseph dies.

Throughout his life Joseph has served and followed God. No matter how bad or cruel he was treated he always trusted God. It was because of this he was promoted and able to overcome difficult times.

WHY WOULD GOD MAKE ANYONE WHO IS A BELIEVER IN HIM LIVE A LIFE WITH SO MUCH TRAGEDY AND TURMOIL?

LIFE LESSONS FROM JOSEPH

Joseph finds himself in a very peculiar position. He had been tied up and sold by his brothers who twenty years later show up needing food. He holds a position of power and can do with his brothers as he pleases. The only thing stopping him is his father. Then when he is fifty-six years old, his father Jacob dies and his brothers go into panic mode. They are afraid Joseph will now get even for all they had done to him. It does not matter how well he is doing, it is about all the pain and suffering he had to go through because of them.[27]

His brothers sent him a note asking for forgiveness and reminding them that this is what father would want him to do.[28] After this his brothers went to him and threw themselves face down on the floor in front of him begging for their lives. Even after all the years they knew what they did was wrong and that it had caused a lot of personal hurt for their brother, Joseph.

Joseph stands above them even as they stood over him when they threw him in the well all those years before. He has the position and power to bring justice and make them pay. Instead as they lay there *"Joseph said to them: "Don't be afraid of me. Am I God, that I can punish you? You intended to harm me, but God intended it all for good. He brought me to this position so I could save the lives of many people. No, don't be afraid. I will continue to take care of you and your children." So he reassured them by speaking kindly to them."*[29]

Joseph has chosen to forgive his brothers. Joseph recognized they had intended to hurt him. He also saw that even in the worst that happens to a believer God is at work guiding and working toward his plans. There are four key lessons we can and should learn from the life of Joseph.

1. Bad things can happen to <u>GOOD</u> people so that God can do <u>GOOD</u> things for the rest of His people. The bad that happened to Joseph was used to save all of Joseph's family and the long range plans of God for a savior were tied to the nation of Israel. Joseph said, *"God intended it all for good."* Everything that happened, even the bad, was going to be used by God and his purpose for good.
2. It is all part of a <u>MASTER</u> plan established by God for each life. We often do not understand how God is working toward a greater goal. God had to move Joseph to Egypt to make sure there would be food for His people in Israel. Everything that happened to Joseph was all intended for a greater purpose. Joseph understood that God *"brought him to this position."*
3. It is about more than just <u>YOU</u>. When you focus on yourself you will not succeed. You will wonder why, instead of why not. God chooses the path so you can be a servant in His kingdom. All that happened to Joseph was *"So I could save many lives."*
4. We have a message of <u>ENCOURAGEMENT</u> to share. Joseph had the power to destroy but he became an encouragement and a positive influence on his family. The believer who can share through the challenges of life about the grace and presence of God will serve as an encouragement to the world around them. Joseph's message to his brothers was *"don't be afraid."*

PAUL OF TARSUS' LIFE JOURNEY

When Paul writes about his life as a believer it is not what you would expect. He had once attacked the followers of

Christ and was confronted by Jesus Himself on the Damascus road.[30] After his conversion Paul became a deeply committed follower of the very one he had denied and fought against. He had been challenged by some believers from Corinth to prove he was a real committed believer. So Paul responded by outlining his credentials and then showing how much he had gone through as a believer.

"But whatever they dare to boast about–I'm talking like a fool again–I dare to boast about it, too. Are they Hebrews? So am I. Are they Israelites? So am I. Are they descendants of Abraham? So am I. Are they servants of Christ?"[31] Paul is a Hebrew's Hebrew with a family lineage that would make any Jew blush with envy. He was willing to say, *"I know I sound like a madman, but I have served him far more!"*[32] He wants them to know how really committed he is to his Lord and Savior.[33] It is a list of all that has happened to him for following Christ.

- *"I have worked harder:* He is not bragging, Paul is about to back this statement up with facts.
- I have *been put in prison more often:* There are not many pastors who brag about being in jail, but we need to remember every time he was arrested it was for his stand for Jesus.
- I have *been whipped times without number:* As people rejected his message Paul would not be quiet or leave and was often attacked and whipped.
- I have *faced death again and again:* It was not a matter of pride or being liked, it was often a matter of almost dying for preaching the truth of Christ.
- *Five different times the Jewish leaders gave me thirty-nine lashes:* This was the strictest punishment the Jews had short of death and Paul had it happen to him five times. This was designed to rip off the flesh. Paul had received 195 lashes of this type. His back was covered with scars and must have looked like a road map for New York City.

- *Three times I was beaten with rods:* A beating with a rod was designed to bruise the muscles deep and to cause pain that lasted for a long period of time.
- *Once I was stoned:* The punishment of stoning was designed to kill a person. That Paul lived through this was a testimony to his will to live. He would have had stones thrown at him until they thought he was dead or dying.
- *Three times I was shipwrecked. Once I spent a whole night and a day adrift at sea:* Traveling with Paul would have been a nightmare. The enemy was throwing anything and everything at him.
- *I have traveled on many long journeys:* These journeys were long and hard trips. Walking from place to place in all sorts of weather, he was faced with all sorts of problems which he spoke about.
- *I have faced danger from rivers and from robbers:* He has had to take on the forces of nature and the forces of evil men who wanted to rob him.
- *I have faced danger from my own people, the Jews, as well as from the Gentiles:* Paul was not going to win any personality contest. He was not out to make friends but to make disciples. The difference was clear to him. He had the ability to make people dislike him because of his commitment to Christ. The concept that believers are to be liked by everyone is contrary to the life of Paul and the life of Jesus.
- *I have faced danger in the cities, in the deserts, and on the seas:* It did not matter where he went, Paul had the ability to find trouble. He also did not let any of it scare him away from his sharing the message of Christ.
- *I have faced danger from men who claim to be believers but are not.* There were false believers and those who turned back to the world who tried to stop his ministry so they could have power in the local churches.
- *I have worked hard and long, enduring many sleepless nights:* Paul was committed and was willing to put in the time to make sure he

succeeded in sharing about Jesus. He also did not let problems stop him from writing to those he was not able to be with.

- *I have been hungry and thirsty and have often gone without food:* It was not about Paul's comfort it was about doing whatever it would take to share the message of Jesus.
- *I have shivered in the cold, without enough clothing to keep me warm:* Paul did not travel in luxury and he did not let the elements stop him.

It is not what most people who are believers see life following Christ like. Many would give up if any one of these happened to them. Paul saw each and every one as a part of the proof of his commitment to Christ. It did not matter what was thrown at him, he was not giving up.

WHY WOULD GOD MAKE ANYONE WHO IS A BELIEVER IN HIM LIVE A LIFE WITH SO MUCH TRAGEDY AND TURMOIL?

LIFE LESSONS FROM PAUL

After all that, how did Paul respond to the other believers? What did he say to encourage them? Paul who had been beaten, lashed, stoned, shipwrecked, robbed, cold, naked, hungry and was not liked by many of the people he came in contact with, was able to put it all into perspective and have some important advice for other believers. What did Paul say about it all?

"And we know that God causes all things to work together for good to those who love God, to those who are called according to His purpose."[34]

Wow, all that bad stuff was actually being used by God for the good of the Kingdom. Paul sounds a lot like Joseph who said, *"God intended it all for good."*

What was Paul able to accomplish?

1. BOOKS written (13): Paul wrote thirteen letters which are included in the New Testament. Romans, 1 Corinthians, 2 Corinthians, Galatians, Ephesians, Philippians, Colossians, Titus, 1 Thessalonians, 2 Thessalonians, 1 Timothy, 2 Timothy, Philemon.
2. CHURCHES started by Paul (Officially around 20): Yet he is in some way responsible for all the churches that have been started in the last 2,000 years.
3. PROBLEMS solved, lives touches: His letters have been the foundation of theological truth for the Christian Church.

All that happened to Paul could not stop him from being used of God and recognizing God was using it all for good. It was for the good of the church Christ was building and Paul did not care what happened to him. He just wanted to serve Jesus. Paul believed *"God causes all things to work together for good"* of the Kingdom.

ETHEL'S LIFE JOURNEY[35]

Her name was Sister Ethel. When I stood in the pulpit, she sat on the front row on my right hand side. She walked very slow and with some pain. She was also one of the greatest prayer warriors I have ever known. Whenever there was a need, everyone in the church and in the local community wanted her to pray for them. That woman knew how to pray. Even as I write that, I realize I never heard her pray out loud. She was a closet prayer warrior. She would take every request to God as if it was the only prayer in the world. She was faithful. If you asked her to pray for you, it was a surety it would happen.

One afternoon I stopped by her singlewide trailer to see how she was doing. She was sitting at the table writing letters. She corresponded with people around the world. They would write sharing prayer needs and problems in their lives. She would answer them and they would go on her prayer list. I had asked her about prayer and how she learned to do it. What I heard was nothing like what I expected and when I left there that day I knew God had sent me and I would never be the same again. I have seen the world much differently since that day. It is one thing to read about Joseph and Paul and say, 'hey, they are Biblical people, they have to meet a higher standard.'

Ethel's father had been very tough on her and as a young girl she had no self-esteem. She had accepted Jesus by reading a gospel tract she found on a train. She left home and began attending church and working at a job she found. After a period of time she meant a young man and fell in love. Even as she told me this her eyes sparkled with the joy of someone who had really been in love and was remembering it. She continued to tell me how their marriage took a turn when he became sick. I cannot remember the sickness or disease he had but it was one that put him in bed and which placed all the responsibilities of care and providing on Ethel. She worked during the day and then took care of him and the house at night. This went on for years and then he died. It was a sad relief. Her husband and friend was gone. His suffering had ended but she was now alone.

After some time she met another man and fell in love and got married. He was a believer and they were very happy. His aged mother who was confined to a wheelchair lived with them and Ethel helped care for her. Then the absolute last thing anyone would have expected happened. Her husband became sick. He grew worse and worse. Finally the doctors found out what was wrong. Her second husband had the same rare sickness her first husband had. Now Ethel was caring for her sick husband, her mother-in-law who was confined to a wheelchair and Ethel had to work to support the three of them. Her days were filled with taking care of other people.

I was shocked as she told the story. Here was the dear lady everyone loved and came to for help and she had lived such a hard and very tragic life. She smiled and said, "Once I almost died. I was sick and was rushed to the hospital. I was in a coma and found myself walking up a flight of stairs toward the clouds. Someone was at the top waiting for me. When I was half-way up I heard my name being called. I did not want to go back down but I stopped and listened. Someone was calling to me. "Ethel come back, don't leave us, we need you." I heard the voice call again and I looked back and suddenly everything was gone. I woke the next day in the hospital with my mother-in-law sitting in her wheelchair next to my bed." She looked at me and said I had almost died and she just started calling me to come back. Ethel looked at me and said, "I really got close to heaven that day."

Sister Ethel told me how she got better and went back to caring for her husband and mother-in-law. The mother-in-law passed away and a few years later her husband died. She had spent most of her life caring for others. Then she told me the why. Why it had all happened. When she was young she had a rough life. Her father was not kind to her. She wanted to run away but instead got saved and went to church. She had taken care of two men. She said all those years she found there was one thing she could do no matter what was happening. She could pray, and pray she did. She told me God had given her those two husbands so she could learn how to pray. She loved to pray. It was God's gift to her and that was also God's gift to everyone she came in contact with.

LIFE LESSON'S FROM SISTER ETHEL

She was called on by friends and strangers to pray for them. Her life was not what any of them could have imagined. Most of their needs were minor in comparison to what she had been through, yet she saw it as her ministry and privilege to pray for each and every one of them.

What do we learn from her life? Do you remember Joseph? The truth from his life applies to the life of Sister Ethel.

1. Bad things can happen to good people so that God can go good things for the rest of His people. "*God*

intended it all for Good." God did not cause the bad to happen but he used it to prepare her for a life of prayer.

2. It is all part of a master plan established by God for each life. "*He brought me to this position.*" She was not mad at God. She saw it as all preparing her to serve God.

3. It is about more than just you. "*So I could save many lives.*" She had touched more lives than any other single person in any church I have pastored.

4. We have a message of encouragement to share. "*Don't be afraid.*" She was a constant encouragement and positive force in the church.

Sister Ether was like Paul. She saw all things working for God when it was put into the hands and plans of God. She did not allow anything to stop her from serving Him. She remained true from the time she read the gospel tract on the train as a young woman through all that happened to her.

A LIFE JOURNEY WITH GOD

Remember I started by saying I was going to tell you the truth? Micaiah the prophet told the truth. It was a hard truth but he told it anyway. I have told you the truth. If you are going to put down a solid foundation it must not be on mush put out by popular preachers who want you to think everything is just going to be hunky dory, peachy keen-o, or just super fine. If you are a believer then God chooses and you follow. He has a plan. It is about the Kingdom of God and the Kingdom of Heaven. It is about Jesus and eternal life. What is in it for you? Well, there is forgiveness and eternal life and an opportunity to be part of the winning team. There is a journey that will turn out for good even if no one understands it, at least understands it yet.

Step one is to change the directions of your life and make a U-TURN. Repent is the opportunity to have your sins forgiven and to join God's team.

Step two is to start your spiritual life trip with God. Faith in God means you are not alone and there is a master plan in place for your life and anything that happens will be used of God for good.

Let me show you how this works. Imagine I put a child in a highchair. Then I get one of those multicolored suckers that are the size of a kitchen plate and I also get a certificate worth one billion dollars printed on plain paper and just black ink and it will not come to maturity for 40 years. Now if I held these up so the child could choose one, which one do you think the child would pick? The devil is holding up a nine inch multi-colored sucker and saying, "take this, enjoy, it won't last long but it is what I have to offer." Meanwhile, God is offering a saving certificate worth eternal life and the forgiveness of all a person's sins. Most people are saying, "I'll take the sugar for a quick high, who cares about tomorrow."

Here is the key for today. When you turn and travel toward God it is a life long journey and it is His master plan for your life which you will be following. If you take this trip you will be richly rewarded. This is putting your FAITH IN GOD! When you do this you will discover *"God causes all things to work together for good to those who love God, to those who are called according to His purpose."*

Learning to Follow Directions

It does not matter if you are driving down the highway or putting together a kids swing set you have to follow directions. There is one Swedish furniture store that has directions which are only pictures. Because they sell their furniture in so many countries they just use pictures and skip the interpretations into all those languages, but they are still directions which need to be followed.

My grandson who is four years old is a fan of Legos. He loves to build them and then tear them apart. Recently I was putting random Lego blocks together when he looked at what I was doing and said, "No grandpa, those don't go together. You need the directions so you know what you are doing." As Christian believers, we need to know God has given us directions to follow. He did this so we would know what we were doing and so we would know it is what God wants us to do.

ADAM AND EVE

They were the first couple, the first people and the first ones ever to get directions from God. The directions were clear and definable. First, they were told they could eat from any tree but one. Second, they were told if they ate from that one tree they would die. Their list of touch and don't touch was simple. The list we have today is a little longer, still a list of touch and don't touch, but it is the same principle. Do certain things and you die or lose any place with God in eternity and lose contact with Him here. When we look at prayer this will be clearly seen as to why some of our prayers are not answered.

There are four clear lists in the New Testament of the DON'T TOUCH items. They are found at 1 Corinthians 6.9-10, Galatians 5.19-21, Ephesians 5.5, and Revelation 21.8.

There are 29 clearly defined items on the lists and, for those who like to think they can skirt God's intentions the 30th one is just for them. It says, and I quote *"and things like these."*[36]

These lists say the same thing: touch or do these and you die or don't get eternal life with God. You don't get to enter the Kingdom of Heaven.

LEARNING FROM ADAM AND EVE

They thought they had it figured out or at least they thought they could get away with it. They believed in God- only not enough to listen to what He had told them. They had four good excuses to use when God did show up.

1. Everyone is doing it! Think about it, literally everyone was doing it. Eve did it. Adam did it and that was everyone. They were all the SAME!
2. It was a private matter between consenting adults. They hid out in the trees with their fig leaves in place. There was no SHAME!
3. It was not hurting anyone! They did not see any consequences for their actions. They could feel no PAIN!
4. It was not their fault! Adam pointed the finger at Eve. Eve pointed the finger at Satan, and Satan had no one to point the finger at. They used the oldest excuse of all. Find someone to BLAME!

Things are not much different today. Now we legalized it, so we can tax it and pay for schools and pot holes. The argument is if we can't stop them we can get some money for something important. What they ignore is the added cost of those who will do it now because it is legal. Driving under the influence of marijuana or as it is called, driving stoned, car crashes are up over 300% in the last decade.[37] This report is before the recent Colorado and Washington State laws legalizing the use of marijuana. You ain't seen nothing yet.

In the garden they did not follow directions and died. They were separated from God because they did not follow the directions. The fellowship was broken and they were cast out to live without the help and benefits of a relationship with God. Jesus came to restore that broken relationship.

THOSE SILLY FOOLS

When the King James Bible was translated and completed in 1611 they had done the best job they could for their time. One of the problems was the translators added some words and expressions to try and help explain the meaning as they interpreted the Bible. An example of this is found in Psalms 14.1. It was translated *"The fool has said in his heart, there is no God."* The problem is, the words 'there is' are not in the original text. The verse actually says, *"The fool has said in his heart, "No, God!""*

The fool does not deny God, he merely looks around and says to God, "NO, GOD!" Like a defiant child, the fool tells the almighty God, "NO!" Now, unlike many modern parents, God will not allow any of His children to tell Him "NO" without paying the consequences.

Janie B Cheaney in her article in the February 22 edition of World Magazine[38] clearly states this position and why it is held. She writes, 'God does not exist' is an intellectual position. No, God! Is a statement of defiance." The world is not intellectually rejecting God, they are just saying "NO!"

I feel most people believe in God, but they also have deliberately chosen to say "NO" to Him and "NO" to his directions for their life. It is not that they don't believe in Him, they just think He is irrelevant to how they will choose to live their life. I remind you what the scripture says again, *"The fool has said in his heart, "No God!"*

WHAT A FOOL SAYS AND THINKS

The world is full of people who are saying "no" to God. They are saying "No, God! You cannot set the rules! We

41

know what the rules are but we will not follow what you say." They are saying, "No, God! I will not listen to you!" They clearly are living their lives in direct disobedience to what they know in their hearts to be God's will. David wrote about such people in the book of Psalms. *"The wicked, in the haughtiness of his countenance, does not seek Him. All his thoughts are, "No, God!""*[39] Look around at this world and see how it shouts to God, NO! The world is full of fools.

Adam and Eve were fools when they ignored what God had told them. Calling them fools here is another way of saying they were disobedient or let's just call it what it is, sin. They believed in God but they did not believe in Him enough to follow the directions He had given them.

SIX FOUNDATIONAL TRUTHS

So far we have looked at the first two of these. First the person is to *repent from dead works*. The individual must make a personal U-turn and head in the direction of God. This is what the prodigal son did when he headed home from feeding the pigs.

Second the person must see their relationship with God as a life long journey. This involves *faith toward God*. In this faith journey God makes the choices and the individual accepts this as all part of God's plan.

The third step is to discover what it means to know *instructions about washings*.

NEW TESTAMENT WASHINGS

The Greek word used for washings is '*baptismos*.' This word is transliterated BAPTISM and it is properly translated WASHINGS. It means to dip or to immerse but is used in a wider sense by the writer of Hebrews. There are four New Testament washings of baptisms. These are about following directions and being obedient to God and following His directions.

WASHING OR BAPTISM BY WATER [40]

This baptism by water had a long tradition. It had been used by the Jews as a proof of conversion. John the Baptist had taken this and changed it to show the repentance of a Jew in returning to the faith and turning from sin. Jesus changed it one more time and made it into a symbol of those who had chosen Him as their Lord and Savior.

Paul wrote about this, explaining it to the church at Rome. He told them baptism or being immersed in water in the name of the Father, Son and Holy Spirit symbolized the death of the individual and the resurrection into new life with Jesus.[41] Peter showed water baptism was also a way to a clear or clean conscience.[42]

Remember washings or baptisms are about following directions and obedience. If you, as a believer in Jesus, have not been baptized you are saying in defiance of His directions to you, "NO, GOD!" You may have some great excuses but you might want to ask Adam and Eve how the excuses worked out for them. It is a vital part of learning to listen and follow the directions of God that you are baptized. There was a time in church history they did not consider you a believer until you had been baptized. At Pentecost Peter told them, *"Repent, and each of you be baptized in the name of Jesus Christ for the forgiveness of your sins; and you will receive the gift of the Holy Spirit."*[43]

WASHING OR BAPTISM OF THE HOLY SPIRIT[44]

Even as John the Baptist was immersing Jews in water he spoke about Jesus and the next washing or baptism. *"I baptized you with water; but He will baptize you with the Holy Spirit."*[45] This washing or baptism would fill the believer with the Holy Spirit or the very presence of God.[46] This Holy Spirit would serve as the individual's guide, counselor and conscience.[47] Without the Holy Spirit, the believer is not able to stand against evil in the spiritual battles he or she will have to face.

WASHING OR BAPTISM OF PERSECUTION[48]

Jesus knew the believer would go through suffering and persecution. *"A slave is not greater than his master. If they persecuted me, they will also persecute you."*[49]

Somehow modern believers have swallowed a lie that followers of Jesus will not suffer and everyone should like them. This then extends to the concept that if people don't like you then you are not a good believer. The opposite is exactly the truth. Paul wrote to the young pastor Timothy, *"Indeed, all who desire to live godly in Christ Jesus will be persecuted."*[50] That means they won't like you and will do bad things to you. This is the baptism of suffering the believer must accept and go through if they want to serve Jesus. This baptism, or washing of persecution or suffering, links us to self-denial and a commitment to Jesus that is designed to keep us holy. It links us to the MINISTRY of Jesus - as He was persecuted, we are also persecuted. It does not matter what the world wants us to believe, we will not be liked by those who reject Jesus as their personal savior.

WASHING OR BAPTISM OF FEET John 13.1-17

Jesus took a common practice of His day and changed its meaning. He washed the feet of his disciples right in the middle of the meal we know as the Last Supper. Then Jesus had a conversation with the disciples about it. He told them, *"If I then, the Lord and the Teacher, washed your feet, you also ought to wash one another's feet."*[51]

The church is divided on what he was talking about. Did he mean for people to literally wash each other's feet? Or, did he mean we are to serve those around us as he did? I believe both are true. It is about obedience and following directions as well as discovering what it is to humble yourself as a follower of the king who became a sacrifice. It is about your surrender and humility and it links the believer to the LIFE of Jesus.

FOOLISH DEFIANCE OR FOLLOWING DIRECTIONS

Eve and Adam had excuses to the excess. They believed in God but not enough to follow the directions He gave them. They learned the hard way there is no excuse for not following the directions given by God. The outcome will be no different for all those today who think they can ignore God's directions and He will just pass them by.

The world is now full of people like Eve and Adam. They believe in God but they are just telling God, "NO!" Eve and Adam were fools for believing they can tell God no and think they would get away with it.

Each believer in Jesus needs to learn to follow directions and be obedient. Learning to follow directions is discovering and participating in the Christian washings or baptisms.

Janie Cheaney in her article titled *'Foolish Defiance'* in World Magazine[52] talks about the excesses of life today and how they are moving this next generation away from God. She writes about the excesses, "Not just too much luxury and debauchery, but too much period: technology; leisure time; diversions; space; also too much insulation from nature, manual work, and practical problem-solving. As the younger generation grows up in an imaginary world mediated through movies and games and electronic community, they can bend the world to suit themselves. Or think they can." They have nothing to do with reality, and have no idea what life is about. Their imaginary world is devoid of God or they think they can be God, doing whatever they want. They think if it is within reach, then there is no reason not to take and enjoy. THEY DO NOT BELIEVE THERE ARE CONSEQUENCES!

We should remember what God said to Job when he was questioning God about all that had happened to him. God sets the stage when he asks Job a long and thought laced rhetorical question.

"Where were you when I laid the foundation of the earth?
Tell Me, if you have understanding,
Who set its measurements? Since you know.
Or who stretched the line on it?
"On what were its bases sunk?
Or who laid its cornerstone,"[53]

WOW! Job had questioned God and the question he got back from God must have knocked his socks off. God asks Job where was here before there was no here? I have always wanted to know that. If there was not a here, then how could God put something here, that did not exist, in a place that was not there? Or here? I'm sure Job did not know the answer and must have looked pretty dumb.

I saw this happen once in a class in college. We had a new professor at the college. He taught the class about the book of Isaiah. It is one of the most controversial and highly debated books in the Bible. It was being taught by Dr. Kenneth Jones. He took roll and handed out the syllabuses. Then it happened! One of the seniors who was taking the class ask Dr. Jones if this was the best book for the class. Now, I was sitting with my book open to the title page of the book and my mouth dropped open. Dr. Jones asked the student what he meant, and the senior continued by telling Dr. Jones he had looked over the book and thought it was too liberal and was not in line with our theological background. I was watching a car wreck happen in slow motion.

Dr. Jones invited us all to open up the book in question. It was the Wesleyan Bible Commentary. He told everyone to turn to the title page and then asked the senior to read the page out loud. I can still hear him read. "The Wesleyan Bible Commentary, Volume Three, Isaiah"[54] his voice was loud and clear but as he continued it trailed off, "by Kenneth E. Jones." There was silence in the class like I have never heard before. He had questioned the authority of the book to the man who had written the book. This is the man who would determine if this senior passed or failed the class. Dr. Jones said, 'thank you,' to what was a stunned and embarrassed senior and then went back to his introductory remarks without saying anything else. The next time we met for class the senior had moved to the far back corner and he never spoke again in that class the entire semester. Knowing Dr. Jones, the senior passed or failed on his class test and papers.

Job has challenged God and God has responded, 'Hey look at the title page and see who the creator is.' Then God adds "*'This far you may come and no farther; here is where your proud waves halt'?*"[55] God is speaking about setting limits on the sea but he is also telling Job, in other words, I wrote the book and I set the rules and I set the limits and you are speaking out of your ignorance.

God is the one who will determine if you pass or fail. It will not be based on if He likes you or not but on whether you are following the directions He has set for life. That is, if you have put down a solid foundation and built on it. Have you made the needed spiritual U-TURN? Have you invited God to travel with you? Are you following the directions? Are you washed in the blood of the lamb?

Believers are called to follow the directions and stay within the rules or boundaries set by God. That is what Christian washings or baptisms are all about. I want to remind you it is His book, He is the author. It is His world, He is the Creator and we are called to follow His directions. If you don't, then you are just an old grandpa who needs to learn how to follow the directions and even a four year old knows that.

Your Position on the Team

It is spring training time again and the home team is beating the other teams down in Arizona. It is when the regular baseball season starts that I get interested. Those are the games that count. It is interesting to me that the players are so specialized. Take the pitcher as an example. He can throw a ball at 85 to 95 mph and get it inside of a strike zone. His goal is to trick the batter into thinking the ball is going somewhere else so the batter will miss the ball.

Here is where it gets interesting. Pitchers are terrible throwers. No, I am not contradicting myself. Pitching and throwing are two different things. It happens all the time, the pitcher has the ball hit back to him and when he tries to throw it the 63 feet to first base, he can't hit the side of a barn, let alone the first baseman's glove. The guy who throws the ball to the catcher with precision cannot even get it near first base, especially if he is in a hurry.

It even gets worse when it comes to batting. Pitchers just cannot bat worth anything. If a pitcher can bat around .165 he is consider a great pitching hitter. There are exceptions but they are few and very far between. Pitchers have the ability to throw the ball at the catcher at incredible speed and accuracy. Then again, they may just not like catchers and are trying to hit them with every pitch. An example of how bad a pitcher can be is "Ron Herbel (who) pitched in 332 games in the 60s and early 70s, mostly for the Giants. He managed only six hits in 227 plate appearances for an anemic .029 batting average."[56] Now it is not entirely their fault. Most pitchers played college ball where there was a DH, or designated hitter, who hit for the pitcher. So a pitcher who comes to the National League where there is no DH is doing something he has not done since he played Pee Wee Baseball.

49

Pitchers, catchers, first base, short stop, second base, third base, outfielders, even Designated hitters, which came into the game in 1973, all have special skills and abilities. They are on the same team but they are not the same. So they are the same only different.

This has spiritual significance for members of the church and the body of Christ.

PERSONAL GIFTS & ABILITIES

"Now there are varieties of gifts, but the same Spirit. And there are varieties of ministries, and the same Lord. There are varieties of effects, but the same God who works all things in all persons."[57]

This is extremely important and simple. I think of all the books written on this subject that have tried to make it complicated and difficult. It is three simple steps all linked together.

There are a variety of GIFTS. In the language of baseball the players have different gifts or abilities. There are those with strong arms, while others have quick reflexes and others have exceptional eye-hand coordination.

There are a variety of MINISTRIES. The guy with the strong arm becomes the pitcher. The guy with the quick reflexes becomes a short stop. The guy with great eye-hand coordination becomes a great hitter.

There are a variety of EFFECTS. The guy with the great arm becomes a pitcher and strikes out the other team. The guy with the quick reflexes who becomes a short stop stops the ball when it is hit to him and gets an out for his team. The guy with the great eye-hand coordination who became a batter or hitter gets runs on the board and helps his team win.

The gifts are matched to ministry and the ministry has intended effects. There may be many gifts but they are

50

given by the same spirit.[58] Each gift is matched to a ministry but it is ministry which you received in the Lord.[59] Even as each gift and matching ministry causes the desired effect it is the same God who causes all things to work together.[60]

These gifts, ministries and the effects they produce are not independent from each other, they are connected. *"Now you are the body of Christ, and each one of you is a part of it."*[61] Using baseball language, now you are on God's TEAM, and each one of you has a position to fill. The gifts are for the benefit of the Kingdom of God and are not for our personal benefits or satisfaction.

BIBLICAL GIFTS

There are four key lists of spiritual gifts in the New Testament.

- Romans 12 list: Encouragement, Giving, Leadership, Mercy, Prophecy, Service, Teaching
- 1 Corinthians 12: Administration, Knowledge, Discernment , Miracles, Healing, Teaching – Teachers, Interpretation of languages, Apostle, Languages, Helps, Prophets – Prophecy, Faith, Wisdom
- 1 Peter 4: Serving, Teaching
- Ephesians 4: Apostles, Evangelists, Pastors, Prophets, Teachers

There is a great debate in the Christian world about how many spiritual gifts there are and how some of them are used. There is no agreement on the exact list. I also believe there are gifts not on the list but which are used and necessary within the Church of the 21st century. We must not limit God in what He can do and in what He will do.

Remember when we looked at how bad pitchers were at hitting? They started allowing designated hitters to bat instead of the pitchers in 1973. The idea was first put forward in 1906 by Connie Mack.[62] Charlie O. Finley, the former owner of the Oakland A's, is quoted as speaking for the designated hitter, ""The average fan comes to the park to see action, home runs. He doesn't come to see a one-, two-, three- or four-hit game. I can't think of anything more boring than to see a pitcher come up, when the average pitcher can't hit my grandmother."[63]

Some people don't see the DH as a part of baseball and others think it adds to the game. I like it, but here is the point. Even if we don't agree on the list, we should use everyone we can to fill the positions in our church. I believe everyone, and I mean everyone has gifts, has a ministry, and should be causing and effecting what is happening because of it.

God wants action in His church and He has different people for different positions just for that reason. If you have a team of all pitchers then where would the hitting be? If you have a team of all fielders than where would the pitching come from?

Some churches are hung up on languages, which is all they do. They preach it, teach it and expect it from everyone in their churches.

Some churches are hung up on healing, that is all they do. Their preacher preaches on it, they teach it all the time and everyone in their churches is expected to be part of the healing ministry.

Some churches are hung up on prophecy. That is all they do. They work overtime to make sure everyone knows what is going to happen at the end of time. They can tell you what they think every image in the book of Revelation means six ways from Sunday.

There are those churches that focus on service to the poor and homeless, and that is basically all they do. Everyone is expected to be dedicated to street people and their causes.

There is usually a reason for this in each church. It is the senior pastor. If the pastor is into languages than he sees his gift as the most important and puts an emphasis on it. If his or her gift is prophecy that may be all the church gets. If he has the gift of service then he will be into the poor and those with special needs.

I served in a church when I first went into ministry where the senior pastor had the gift of evangelism. He just wanted to win people to Jesus. It was his gift and his heart. He expected everyone in the church to be an evangelist. He taught classes and required every staff member to go out and try and reach strangers with the message of Jesus. Every Monday night we would meet at the church and go out and knock on doors and evangelize. The whole church was learning how to be catchers and every position on his church team was geared toward catchers or being an evangelist. This is in direct opposition to the Word of God.

Paul wrote to the Ephesian church about this very matter. "*And He gave **some** as apostles, and **some** as prophets, and **some** as evangelists, and **some** as pastors and teachers.*"[64] They have different gifts and need to be aware that everyone does not have their gift. Even among the church pastors there are different types. Some throw fast balls and some curve balls. Some are knuckle ball throwers and some are just knuckle heads expecting everyone on their team to have the same gift they have.

Now, this is like a baseball team just using pitchers to fill every position on the field. It is getting the best catchers and putting them on all the bases and in the outfield, even using one to pitch. He would probably pitch from his knees wearing all those pads. NOT GONNA WORK, but that is how some pastors and churches operate.

I have the gift of teaching and preaching, at least I think I do, and I have to be careful that is not all we do in the church I pastor. I have to be careful that I don't just get the church to sit around and listen to me teach. That would make me feel good because I would be using my gift but then no one else would be using theirs. No matter what gift a pastor has, he or she has to be careful not to limit the church to ministry according to that gift.

So, as the pastor I have responsibilities. A lot happens that I am responsible for, but I am not the whole team, I am a member of the team. I have to remember that and so do the members of the church.

Here is where it gets messy some times. Let's say the pastor is the pitcher on the team and he is the only one who goes out on the field. Here is what it would look like. He winds up and pitches the ball and it is a strike, but there is no catcher, he is in the dugout sitting on the bench. The pitcher has to run back and get the ball. He does this a couple of times but then the batter hits the ball and it goes into the outfield. Since there is no outfielder, the pitcher has to run out to get the ball and try and run down the guy who hit the ball. Then when the games is over the players in the dugout get together and decide what they need is a new pitcher so they don't lose any more games. Sounds silly but that is how some churches operate. They expect the pastor to do it all.

That is not how it is supposed to be. *"Now you are the body of Christ, and each one of you is a part of it."*[65]

Now you are God's TEAM, and each one of you has a position to fill. When we see this and do this we will discover what it means to become a winning team and part of a growing church.

SIX FOUNDATIONAL TRUTHS

It is important to see how the laying of hands fits into the six basic or foundational teachings.

1. Repentance from Dead Works: This is about starting the Christian life by making a personal 'you turn.'

2. Faith toward God: This is about a life long journey. Salvation is the beginning of our time with God and must be followed by a committed life.
3. Instructions about Washings: Means we as believers are learning to follow directions. Our life is about discovering what it means to be obedient to God.
4. Laying on of Hands: Is about finding your position on the TEAM! This is where we discover our gifts, ministry and have an effect for God.
5. Resurrection of the Dead: The surprise about being alive.
6. Eternal Judgment: Will complete our journey

LAYING ON OF HANDS

There are six basic New Testament reasons for the Laying on of Hands. Each of them ties us to ministry and service.

- There is the laying on of hands for a BLESSING
  - This is about POSITIVE SUPPORT: *"People were also bringing babies to Jesus to have him touch them. When the disciples saw this, they rebuked them. But Jesus called the children to him and said, "Let the little children come to me, and do not hinder them, for the kingdom of God belongs to such as these. I tell you the truth, anyone who will not receive the kingdom of God like a little child will never enter it."*[66]
- There is the laying on of hands for HEALING
  - This is about PRAYERFUL INTERCESSION: Jesus said his followers would *"lay hands on the sick, and they will recover."*[67]
- There is the laying on of hands for SERVICE
  - This is about PERSONAL RESPONSIBILITIES: Six had been chosen to serve the widows and handle a dispute within the church. *"These they brought before the apostles; and after praying, they laid their hands on them."*[68]

- There is the laying on of hands to receive the HOLY SPIRIT.
  - This is about POWERFUL FILLING: Paul found some believers at Ephesus who had not heard of the Holy Spirit. *"When Paul had laid his hands upon them, the Holy Spirit came on them."*[69]
- There is the laying on of hands for Spiritual LEADERS.
  - This is about PASSING ON MINISTRY: This was what Paul was warning Timothy about when he wrote, *"Do not lay hands upon anyone too hastily and thereby share responsibility for the sins of others."*[70] A young minister's call is recognized through the laying on of hands of the other ministers.
- There is the laying on of hands for Spiritual GIFTS.
  - This is about PUBLIC RECOGNITION: *"For this reason I remind you to kindle afresh the gift of God which is in you through the laying on of my hands."*[71]

These are all about being part of the team. They are about gifts, ministry and effects God intends for his followers. *"Now there are varieties of gifts, but the same Spirit. And there are varieties of ministries, and the same Lord. There are varieties of effects, but the same God who works all things in all persons."*[72]

There is a <u>Variety of Gifts</u>. Every believer has a gift or gifts that are to strengthen the Team/Church. There is a <u>Variety of Ministries</u>. Each gift is linked to a purpose or ministry to help others and benefit the church. There is a <u>Variety of Effects</u>. This is the results of using the gifts for the ministries they were intended for.

These all link us spiritually. The same Spirit determines the gifts each one is to receive. The same Lord is served by the ministry and the same God has a master plan that He wants us to be part of. The church is God's team and we are all called to discover and fill our positions on the team.

So when the ball is hit it is not the pitcher running to the outfield to recover it, but an outfielder who snags the fly. It is not the pitcher who is swinging the bat, but the designated hitter who is filling his or her spot on the team.

The laying on of hands is about ministry. It is about being on God's team and WINNING!!!!!

The Next Step

There is a transition between life and eternal life that we take for granted, but which is vital if we are going to understand our life journey as believers and followers of Christ Jesus. This is not about eternal judgment. This is about making the transition or moving from life to eternal life. Often this next step and eternal judgment are combined as one, but the writer of Hebrews was very clear that this is one of the six steps of the believer's life.

I do not like to fly. I am not afraid of flying; I just do not like the experience. It all starts long before you ever get to the airplane. You show up and have to check in your baggage, which you may never see again. Then comes the security lines. You are herded like cattle so you can eventually get to the counter where you remove your coat, shoes, hats, belts and are scanned for any forbidden objects. Twice I have also gotten the full body pat down. That is just wrong that strangers are allowed to do that to you in front of half the people in the world. Then you get to proceed to the gate where you get to wait for your airplane. The only thing that can make it worse is what happened to me on one of my trips back east when I was working on my master's degree. I arrived at the airport with just an hour before my plane was due to take off. I went to the ticket counter and handed her my ticket and driver's license. She looked at me and asked if I would wait. Then she took my ticket and driver's license over to a person who was obviously a supervisor. When they returned I was told my driver's license was out of date. My birthday had been the month before and I had somehow missed getting it renewed. According to federal guidelines it was no longer a valid I.D. After several fearful minutes and several phone calls, I was told I would be able to board after a thorough search. What happened next was right out of the book "1984." I was told to wait. They would send a message out and my bags would be inspected before being put on the plane. I found out that meant my bags would be removed from the cart and brought back to the main area to be searched. They were opened and ransacked. While this was taking place my adventure began. The lady behind the counter closed her station even though there was a long line and walked me around to security. I was walked passed everyone to an empty, closed security line. I was told to wait again. Then they brought people from another security line over and along with an armed guard and the lady from the ticket counter at the front. I watched as my carry on and my computer cases were all emptied on the counter. Every item was gone through and examined. I looked around and everyone was looking at me. Here I stood in my sock feet, holding up my pants because they had my belt, while 6 or seven people went through my stuff. Then they turned to me. I was scanned, patted down and questioned. Finally after about fifteen minutes I was cleared to go on. All so I could be crammed into a seat designed for someone who obviously was much smaller and bent at different places than I do.

I dreaded the trip back because I saw this happening again or worse they could just say tough luck and make me walk home. I arrived at the airport on the east coast early dreading the coming experience. I handed the lady my ticket and my driver's license. She looked at both, smiled and said. "Sir, you driver's license is out of date, you might want to get it updated before the police pull you over and give you a ticket. Have a nice flight." She handed me my ticket and driver's license and sent me on my way.

Now this is more than just a story. Some people come to death's door and it is like arriving at the airport in Seattle. It is filled with drama and yet others arrive at death's door and they pass through smoothly. Some linger sick and dying for days, months or even years, and others just up and die. There is one thing for sure, we all are going to have to face the fact that it is coming.

Then there are the few who think they can escape all this. They see their death as temporary and reversible. They are the people who are being cryogenically frozen. The first one was Dr. James Bedford who was frozen on January 12th, 1967. Time magazine ran an article about him with the title of the article about the event: "Never Say Die."[73]

The most famous person ever cryogenically frozen was the baseball player Ted Williams. He died on July 5, 2002. His body was taken to Scottsdale, Arizona to be frozen. This is where it gets weird. His head was removed and frozen in a separate container. "The head is stored in a steel can filled with liquid nitrogen. It has been shaved, drilled with holes and accidentally cracked 10 times."[74] Some reports say it was accidentally dropped. The cost of the procedure was $136,000. If Ted is ever brought back to life, the first problem he will have after being revived is discovering he needs to find his body. He will need to pay $111,000 to the people who froze him. The family has not paid the full bill.

Now, I contend that no matter how hard you try to hang on to this life, when it is over, it is over. Ted's head and body may be in Arizona but the rest of Ted has moved on. What happens is what I want to talk about. Hebrews calls it the resurrection of the dead. I call it the 'to' factor.

6 FOUNDATIONAL TRUTHS

1. Repentance from Dead Works
    Making a personal YOU TURN
2. Faith toward God
    Life long JOURNEY
3. Instructions about Washings
    Learning to follow DIRECTIONS
4. Laying on of Hands
    Discovering your PURPOSE for life
5. Resurrection of the Dead
    You are CHANGED Forever!
6. Eternal Judgment

It is this fifth step we will focus on. What happens between life and eternal life? It may take only a moment, a mere twinkling of an eye but it is important.

LUKE 16.19-31

Jesus was a master story teller. He often used parables or made up stories to illustrate His point. There were also times when He was not telling a story but was talking about real people. This happened when He started talking about resurrection of the dead and eternal life.

It was not a parable but about real people. He does not name the one man because he may have had family members who would recognize him. Jesus knew the name of the man. He also knew the other man. Lazarus was a common name in his time. Yet, Jesus knew all about this Lazarus. What happened to these two men will help us understand what happens at death's door.

Though their fate is talked about here, I want to focus only on what happens at death and not at the judgment. These are two distinct things. We will cover how each ended up where they did in the next chapter, but for now we need to see the transition that takes place when a person dies.

The story is simple. There were two men. One man was rich. He lived a life of luxury. He died and went to hades. The other man was poor and suffered. His name was Lazarus. He died and went to heaven.[75]

TRANSITION

There is a transition we all will have to go through. This transition is moving from life 'TO' eternal life. This 'TO' is all about death and dying of our bodies. This 'TO' is what we are going to look at in great detail. This is about passing through what has been called 'death's door.' You step through and when you do, a lot happens in a twinkling of an eye. I just want to go over this quickly. I have some key things you need to know. Knowing these will not change what happens but it may make it easier for you to live and be ready for what is coming next.

FACT #1

Everyone, everywhere is going to <u>Die</u>.[76]

This applies to the rich and the poor. It applies to believers and non-believers.[77] This was true of the rich man and it was true of Lazarus.

FACT #2

Death is a <u>Door</u> and not a <u>Nap</u>.

Death is often described as sleeping and is even spoken of in scripture of this way. This is a point of perspective and not the fact in the matter. Paul spoke of this in his letter to the church at Corinth. *"Listen, I tell you a mystery: We will not all sleep, but we will all be changed."*[78] At every funeral where the casket is open, someone will always say of the dead person, 'He looks just like he is asleep.' First that is not true. Second, if I look like that when I am asleep throw some dirt on me and get on with your life. Finally, it is about our point of perspective. The closest thing to how a person looks when they are dead is described as sleeping.

When people die they pass through the door, even if it looks like they are asleep to those of us who are left behind. This was true of the thief on the cross who called on Jesus for help. Jesus told him he would be in Paradise[79], or the third heaven where God lives, on that very day. That day he passed through death's door and found out he was not asleep but in heaven.

Jesus was clear about the matter to the Sadducees. They thought there was no life after death. Jesus, who had been in heaven, knew differently. Jesus reminded them about what the scriptures say. *""But regarding the resurrection of the dead, have you not read what was spoken to you by*

God: 'I AM THE GOD OF ABRAHAM, AND THE GOD OF ISAAC, AND THE GOD OF JACOB'? He is not the God of the dead but of the living."[80] Abraham, Isaac, and Jacob were not asleep, they were alive with God.

There were also the rich man and Lazarus. The rich man was in hades and Lazarus was in heaven while five brothers of the rich man were still alive on earth.[81] The rich man and Lazarus were not asleep; they had passed through death's door into eternal life for Lazarus, and eternal punishment for the rich man.

When John, the son of Zebedee, was imprisoned on the Isle of Patmos he was given a vision. In that vision he saw in heaven "a great multitude which no one could count, from every nation and all tribes and peoples and tongues, standing before the throne and before the Lamb, clothed in white robes." These were people who had died and as believers received eternal life. They were in heaven and not asleep. They were not taking a nap, they had passed through the door marked death.

So when Paul wrote, "We believe that Jesus died and rose again and so we believe that God will bring with Jesus those who have fallen asleep in him." They are asleep to us but they are alive to Jesus and will come with Him when he comes for us.

FACT #3

When a person dies, the physical body is replaced with a spiritual body.[82]

The physical bodies we now have are not made to last and cannot enter into eternity. They are perishable bodies and must be replaced with imperishable bodies.[83] We all grow old and discover that we cannot do the things we used to do. In some cases it even crosses over to what can be called dishonor.[84] Just visit any nursing home and see what happens to some who can no longer care for themselves. They can expect to receive bodies that will replace the dishonor with glory. The weakness of human flesh will be replaced with the power of a body that will never die or grow old.[85]

These physical bodies are only temporary and are not meant to transition over to the spiritual world.

FACT #4

You will be upgraded to face the eternal God. Flesh and blood (physical) cannot inherit the Kingdom of God (spiritual).[86] It is important to know that everyone will be changed when they die.[87]

FACT #5

99.99% of the time it is a one-way trip. It seems like every other day someone is writing a book about going to heaven and then coming back to give us some information. There is one really big problem with this. 99.99% of the time they contradict scripture.

When we look at the Old Testament there are only three people who came back from the dead. First, there is the widow of Zarephath whose son Elijah raised from the dead.[88] Second there was the Shunamite's son raised by Elisha.[89] Finally there was the man who was brought back to life when his body was tossed into the grave with the bones of Elisha.[90]

In the New Testament there are also a few raised from the dead. Jesus raised the widow of Nain's son.[91] He raised the twelve year old daughter of Jairus, the Synagogue ruler, back to life.[92] He raised the brother of Mary and Martha, Lazarus, back to life after he had been dead four days.[93] When Jesus died, the graves of many saints around Jerusalem were opened and they came back to life to testify about Jesus.[94]

Peter raised Tabitha, also known as Dorcas, back to life.[95] Euthychus was raised back to life by Paul.[96] There are just eight individuals who are named as having been brought back to life and a handful more at the resurrection of Jesus who are not named. This, in contrast to the billions who have lived and died over all of history, means saying 99.99% may be understating the numbers who have not come back from the dead.

FACT #6

These new bodies are given to everyone.[97] The scriptures are clear, "*Behold, I tell you a mystery; we will not all sleep, but we will all be changed.*" This is true of the righteous and the unrighteous, saints and sinners. There are some who what us to believe otherwise.

In the book "Heaven is for Real"[98] a little four year old is supposed to have gone to heaven for three minutes. When he returns he has a lot to say about heaven. He claims Jesus told him only the righteous get new bodies when they die. He says the bad people don't get new bodies when they die. This is contrary to the Word of God. We may not all die but we all will be changed. On this the scriptures are clear. I point this out in my book "Is This Heaven for Real?"[99] It comes down to the questions: Do you make decisions based on feelings or on facts? Do you make decisions based on rumors or on truth? Do you make decision based on what people say or on what the inspired Word of God says? If you want to make decisions based on feelings and rumors and what people say, you will believe a four year old who says Jesus told him only the righteous get new bodies. If you want to make decisions based on facts and truth and the Word of God, then you will know that everyone, the righteous and the unrighteous, get new bodies before they stand before God at the end of their lives.

FACT #7

These new bodies are designed so they will last forever! We must remember heaven is forever and hades is forever.

Those who go to heaven will be there forever and those who go to hades will be there forever.

There are plenty who want to disagree with me on this. The only problem is they are not disagreeing with me. They are actually disagreeing with Jesus. Jesus said of judgment, *"Then they will go away to eternal punishment, but the righteous to eternal life."*[100] I cannot put enough emphasis that I did not say this but Jesus said it as clearly and distinctly as possible. There is eternal life and eternal punishment. This is the reason there are eternal bodies. They will have to last forever.

Some want to argue that God would not send anyone to Hades forever. We will cover why in the next chapter in great detail but for now, let us just consider the one key fact. Anyone who has rejected the Son of God has rejected his death and suffering for them. They have caused the Father the greatest pain there is. To reject His son is to choose eternal punishment. Jesus clearly warned about this. Yet, there are many, including some preachers, who want to say otherwise. These are people I do not want to stand next to in the judgment.

THE RESURRECTION OF THE DEAD

This sixth step in the life of a believer is a transition from life to eternal life. There are seven simple facts about this we need to know and understand.

1. Everyone will experience it.
2. Death is a Door not a Nap.
3. The Spiritual will replace the Physical.
4. This is an upgrade preparing us to face God.
5. 99.99% of the time it is a one-way trip.
6. Everyone gets a new body.
7. These new bodies will last forever.

When it is over you can bury your body or you can cremate it. You can freeze it, with or without the head attached. You can shoot it out into space like Gene

Roddenberry, the creator of Star Trek, and his wife Majel Barrett, who played Christine Chapel in the original Star Trek series, did with their bodies. It does not matter; you will get a new body. That does not depend on how good or how bad you are. This is about the transition and not about the final destination. This is about being past the last opportunity to make any changes in your ticket and just before you spend eternity at your assigned location.

The scriptures say *"we will all be changed."*[101] It will happen so fast the Bible describes it as happening *"in the twinkling of an eye."* After this we face the final judgment. This is what we will look at next. I might warn you to fasten your seatbelts, make sure your tray tables are put away and that you seats are in their upright position, because for some of you, it is about to be a very bumpy and unpleasant trip.

One FINAL Appointment

There are really only two types of people when it comes to appointments. There are those who are on time and those who are basically, never, ever on time. The ones who arrive on time are driven crazy by the ones who are always late. It happens in every family with at least two people. There will be one waiting at the door while the other one is taking care of last minute details that the other one did an hour before. One of my children used to drive me up a wall when he was small and living at home. He was always late. We even tried telling him a different time so he could be late in his mind and on time for us. It worked twice and then he caught on. From then on he was super late.

Then there is the time you have to spend in a doctor's office. You have an appointment but that is to get you there. There is no telling how long you have to wait to get into an examine room where you will get to wait again. It is like waiting on a ride at Disneyland except without the ride at the end.

There is coming one appointment everyone will be on time for. They cannot be late and they cannot arrive early. This one final appointment is after death when a person gets their eternal body and before they begin their assigned place in eternity. This one final appointment is the last of the steps the writer of Hebrews called the foundations or the elementary teachings of the Christian faith.

ETERNAL APPOINTMENTS Luke 16.19-31

Jesus told about two men He personally knew about. One of them died and went to heaven. The other one died and went to hades. They were separated from each other for eternity. The one who went to hades was suffering in great torment. Since he could not get out of hades he wanted to get word to his five brothers who were still alive on earth.

We can gather several important facts from this instance told to us by Jesus. First, when people die, they do not sleep or take a nap; they pass through death's door to the other side. They get new bodies and then they face the judgment of God. From there they either go to heaven or hades forever. They have passed the point of no return and have reached their last appointment. Why they each went to a different destination is what we need to discover.

THREE THINGS YOU NEED TO KNOW

Life can be broken down into three parts for the believer and the non-believer. First there is the JOURNEY. This is where the decisions are made. The decision is either to follow Jesus or not to follow Jesus. Everyone without Jesus is lost and needs to be found. This was why Jesus came in the first place. He came to *"seek and to save what was lost."*[102] He knew a person could make choices until they got to the TRANSITION and then it would be too late. It is at the transition where a *"man is destined to die once, and after that to face judgment."*[103] This passing from life to eternal life happens in a twinkling of an eye but a lot happens. This is preparing the person for their eternal DESTINATION which happens right after one final appointment with God. Jesus was clear about the judgment. It is *"then* [the unrighteous] *will go away to eternal punishment, but the righteous to eternal life."*[104]

The JOURNEY covers the first four steps of the foundation we have been looking at. The opportunity to take a personal U-turn is available. Those who do are making a commitment to a lifelong trip with God. During this trip they have to follow directions and find their place on the team so they can do their part.

The TRANSITION is when each person reaches the point of no return. This is about changing and leaving the physical behind and moving into the spiritual world, forever.

Then there is the DESTINATION. This is what life is really about. Life is only about where we will end up for eternity.

Most people ignore this or deny it will happen but they cannot avoid it. It is coming.

What I want to do is look at each one briefly and show you how they are linked.

THE JOURNEY

We are all on a life journey toward one last appointment with God. Some people take the time to get ready and make the necessary preparations and some don't do anything. One thing we can know is Jesus has provided the only way for us to be ready to meet God.

Jesus *"came to seek and to save what was lost."*[105] He wanted us to understand how important this was to Him and to His heavenly father. He told three parables back to back to back to highlight this point. First, there was the one about the lost sheep.[106] It had wandered away and the shepherd left the other ninety-nine and went looking everywhere. He was willing to risk his life to find it no matter how far it had strayed away. When he found it he rejoiced and threw a party to celebrate the return of the lost sheep. Second, there was the parable of the lost coin.[107] It was part of a dowry and was extremely important to the woman. When she realized it was gone she tore the house apart looking for it. When she found it she was so overjoyed she asked all her friends in to celebrate the finding of the lost coin. The final parable was about a lost son.[108] He had left his father and went away to live his life in sinful and wasteful ways. When he came to his senses and returned home his father was watching for him. The father was so overjoyed that he threw a banquet.

Each of the parables has the same three elements. Something is lost, which gets found and then everyone celebrates. Jesus came looking for the lost souls of those who were estranged, through sin, from the Father. His goal is to find them and to celebrate. Jesus *"Christ was sacrificed once to take away the sins of many people; and he will appear a second time, not to bear sin, but to bring salvation to those who are waiting for him.*"[109] He knew it was not enough to find the lost; he had to make a way to get them back to the father. He took their sins, our sins, and through His death provided a way we could return to the father even as the prodigal son did. Jesus knew what joy that brought to the Father. It was in each parable.

The individual needs to know this was not an afterthought or something God thought up at the last minute. It is part of his master plan. Long before we were born God put it all into motion. *"But God demonstrates his own love for us in this: While we were still sinners, Christ died for us."*[110] Here is where many want to avoid the truth of their very nature without God. We *"all have sinned and fall short of the glory of God."*[111] It is not that some needed Christ to die for them. It is what we all need. *"We have redemption through His blood, the forgiveness of our trespasses, according to the riches of His grace"*[112]

I love a good bargain. I look forward to the summer and yard sale season. My wife and I enjoy the Saturday morning hunt for the bargain. Since we have grandchildren it has added something new to the hunt. Toys for the grandkids are always high on our list at yard sales. Even when prices are listed we will try and get it cheaper. This is exactly opposite of what Jesus did for us as sinners. The price that was listed is clear. *"The wages of sin is death."*[113] He did not get us by being beaten with twenty lashes or an hour on the cross. It cost Him His life to set us free from sin. The word 'redeem' means to 'pay the full price' and that is exactly what Jesus did for each of us.

As we accept Him and change the direction of our journey we discover three very important truths about Him and following Him. First, He is <u>the way</u>, not just one of many ways. There are those who want us to believe there are many ways to God. They see truth as relative and changing. Truth is final and absolute. Truth is actually a person. Grasping this truth is the key to life, eternal life.

Jesus said, *"I am THE way and THE truth and THE life. No one comes to the Father except through me."*[114] He is not a way but *the way*. He is not some truth, in Him is all real truth about what is eternal. It is through Him a person discovers eternal life and a relationship with the Father.

THE TRANSITION

This Journey is about a way of life that relies on Jesus and His relationship with God the Father. Each person, those with Jesus and those without Jesus, are on a journey and they all have one thing in common. That journey will end at a transition point. We will all die or fly up to meet him in the air, but our lives here on earth will end. Those who live long enough will eventually die. The only thing that will stop is if Jesus returns. Then everyone will be changed.[115] In either case the perishable will put on imperishable. The weakness and dishonor of this life and our physical bodies will be replaced with glory and strength of spiritual and eternal bodies. This is true of saints and sinners alike. It is vital to know these new bodies are eternal and are designed to be used forever. They are the bodies we will face God with at the judgment.

THE DESTINATION

Those who die on an individual basis will face God and receive their eternal rewards or punishment right after they get these new bodies. That leaves those who are alive when Jesus returns and brings time to a close. They will not die but they will be changed. The United States Census Bureau estimates that the world population exceeded 7 billion on March 12, 2012.[116] Each year, the world's population grows by about 80 million. If it continues to grow at such a rate the world's population will reach 9 billion by the year 2035.[117] There are more people alive today than have lived in all of history combined. That means the judgment at the end of time will be a big deal with half of humanity discovering on the same day where they will spend eternity. *"We must all appear before the judgment seat of Christ, that each one may receive what is due him for the things done while in the body, whether good or bad."*[118] Everyone will make one last stop before eternal life. That stop is before God Almighty. This is not an opportunity for mercy; it is where justice is delivered. God does not send people to heaven or hades. He honors the decisions they made while alive on earth in physical bodies. It is here at the judgment seat of God that the unrighteous *"will go away to eternal punishment, but the righteous to eternal life."*[119]

Those who want to say that no one goes away to punishment have one small problem. It was Jesus who said at the end the unrighteous *"will go away to eternal punishment, but the righteous to eternal life."*[120] If you want to say he was wrong then you are saying you don't believe Him. If you say He was right then there is coming a separation of those who serve and follow Jesus from those who have rejected or ignored His call.

Recently my grandson was over with his mother and brother. The little guy got in trouble and was taken to a three minute timeout. He started acting up and his mom said it could become a five minute timeout if he kept it up. He was not happy for all three minutes. Then the three minutes was up and he was released. This is important: his mother said three minutes and that was how long it was. Jesus said both punishment and life with God would be eternal. How long is eternal? Eternal is forever.

There are four lists[121] in the New Testament of what people without Jesus do with their lives. Their lives demonstrate they are without Him and don't care. These lists are extensive and cover every possible form of sin. We live in a society that is ignoring these and even saying they are no longer wrong or sinful. Here is the catch. When I am driving down the highway and everyone is doing 75 MPH and I go along so I don't get run over, does that mean I am not speeding, or does it mean everyone is speeding?

Just because everyone is doing it does not mean it is not sin. Even if people start spray painting signs that read 60 mph to read 75 mph that does not change the speed limit. It is set. Either you are with Jesus or you aren't. If you are with Him, then your life will reflect it. If you aren't, then your life will reflect the items on the lists.

Heaven is a place that is perfect. It always has been and always will be. *"Nothing impure will ever enter* [heaven], *nor will anyone who does what is shameful or deceitful, but only those whose names are written in the Lamb's book of life."*122 To get into heaven, reservations are required and there are no exceptions. Remember, Jesus said He was the ONLY way. A lot of people are going to show up and be very surprised when they don't get into heaven.

This final step in the life of a believer is one of joy and rewards. It is why Jesus came. It is why the believer lives their life in obedience and follows the rules and guidelines set up by God.

IRA's

Each and every person needs to pay attention to their IRA's. I am not talking about Individual RETIREMENT Accounts. I am talking about Individual RESURRECTION Accounts. This is about making the preparations necessary to come before God. The rich man was not ready and he found himself cut off from God and heaven forever. Jesus called it *'eternal punishment'* for a reason. It lasts forever. Lazarus who sat at his gate in life had his Individual RESURRECTION Account all ready and discovered that 'eternal life' was forever.

Each person is on a journey through life. Some are making preparations for eternal life and some are ignoring the future. When a person has made the transition and passed through death's door, the only thing left is finding out where they are going to spend eternity and that should not come as any real surprise to anyone.

Jesus is *"THE way and THE truth and THE life. No one comes to the Father except through"*123 Him.

One of the real tragedies of many believers is they miss the joy of the trip. I have known too many believers who act like they are mad at God for interrupting their lives and causing them to give up so much. Yet when examined, there is nothing that is beneficial that a believer is asked to give up or not take on this journey with them.

WHAT NOT TO TAKE

"*Put to death, therefore, whatever belongs to your earthly nature: sexual immorality, impurity, lust, evil desires and greed, which is idolatry. Because of these, the wrath of God is coming. You used to walk in these ways, in the life you once lived. But now you must rid yourselves of all such things as these: anger, rage, malice, slander, and filthy language from your lips.*"[126]

When my family went on a trip, as a child there was one thing I knew for sure, we could not take everything in the car we had at the house. That is also true of our spiritual journey. There are some things we cannot take with us if we plan to go all the way and to have a good trip.

A believer has to practice personal holiness if they are going to have a successful trip. That means there are items or behaviors that cannot be part of the life of one who is living for Jesus. These items are described as part of the person's "*earthly nature.*" These are the same items most of the world is focused on for their entertainment and satisfaction. These things must be "*put to death.*" They cannot be cut back on or controlled. They must be completely eliminated from the life of the believer in all forms.

There are also some things that must come under the control of the believer. This means it is a personal choice to "*rid yourself*" of them. This is about daily choices that the believer has to make. Will the person control their anger or will they let their anger control them. This is also true of "*malice, slander, and filthy language.*" These items must not be part of the life of a believer. You don't get to take them along on the trip with you.

HOW TO TREAT EACH OTHER

"Do not lie to each other, since you have taken off your old self with its practices and have put on the new self, which is being renewed in knowledge in the image of its Creator. Here there is no Greek or Jew, circumcised or uncircumcised, barbarian, Scythian, slave or free, but Christ is all, and is in all."[127]

Our words about and to each other must be filled with truth. We must not lie or blaspheme about each other. Believers need to remember we are not only going to spend the rest of our lives together, we are also going to spend eternity together. That we speak only positive uplifting words about each other is vital. It is like being in the back seat of the car on a long trip. You can either be bothered by everything the other person does or you can enjoy the trip together.

A great part of this is remembering we are all equal in God's sight. Paul goes to great lengths to make sure we understand this simple fact. Since there are things you have already removed from your life that would make you act negatively toward others, you must not allow them back in. Each believer should be seen as God sees them.

In the family of God there is *"no Greek or Jew."* That means there are no national differences in the family of God. In Paul's day, to be a Roman citizen put you above others in the empire. Paul had a long list supporting his national background including that he was *"of the people of Israel."*[128] Paul wanted the believers to know it did not make any difference to God and it should not make any difference to them.

In the family of God there is no *"circumcised or uncircumcised."* Your religious background is not important. Paul was a Hebrew *"circumcised on the eighth day.*" He had been raise from birth as a dedicated Jew. He was "*of the tribe of Benjamin, a Hebrew of Hebrews; in regard to the law, a Pharisee.*"[129] Yet he counted it as nothing as far as being part of the family of God. Religious or non-religious, it does not matter; what matters is your relationship with Christ.

It does not matter if the believer was a barbarian. This was Paul's way of making reference to someone who was devoid of values and had lived a sinful lifestyle before being saved. Paul said they could even be a Scythian and when they became a believer they were equal to all other believers. A Scythian made a barbarian look like a Sunday school teacher. They were the worst of the worst.

Sometimes in the church we see people differently and do not accept the forgiveness Christ has provided for them. I was faced with this several years ago in one of the churches I pastored. I had a church member set up an appointment with me. When he arrived he had another man with him. He told me his friend wanted to come to church but three other churches had already turned him away. The man had molested a family member years before. He had served his jail sentence and while in jail had accepted Jesus as his personal savior.

I found myself between two responsibilities. The one was the church I pastored and my responsibility to protect them and their families. The other was to accept the forgiveness that Jesus has promised to anyone, even someone who had molested a family member. I approached the leadership of the church and we came up with a solution that covered both bases. The man was allowed to attend church but he was not allowed anywhere in the building alone. There were five people who knew of the circumstances and the man was not allowed to go anywhere without one of them being with him. When I told him he could go to church, tears welled up in his eyes. I had no doubt he was a born again believer. He had been a Scythian. We may not agree on the worst sins or the ones we find it hard to forgive, but they do exist. These are the worst of the worst and when they are forgiven they are equal in the eyes of God. That is also the way we are supposed to see them. There is no limit to God's love and forgiveness.

There is no slave or free in the family of God. Most slaves in the Roman Empire had sold themselves into the position. They were willing to serve as a slave for food, shelter and protection. This placed them on the lower order of the financial society. Those who owned slaves were on the upper end of the financial spectrum. Yet, people who are born again are not categorized according to their financial status. At least they are not supposed to be categorized or viewed by how much they have or don't have.

I have only known two millionaires in my time as a minister. One of them was put into leadership by the church members because he was so rich. He wanted to run the church but he barely gave anything to support it. He had been elected to his position because of his financial status and not because he had a relationship with God. Paul was warning this was the wrong attitude.

When writing to the church at Galatia Paul added one other item to this list. Paul wrote there was neither "*male nor female.*"[130] The gender barriers of the world and those put up by some believers are not the same ones God uses. He sees all the same and wants believers to see each other as equals in the family of God. "*Christ is all, and is in all.*" We have to remember there are no barriers or different levels of believers. We are to treat each other as equals in the family of God.

WHAT TO PACK & WEAR

"*Therefore, as God's chosen people, holy and dearly loved, clothe yourselves with compassion, kindness, humility, gentleness and patience. Bear with each other and forgive whatever grievances you may have against one another.*

Forgive as the Lord forgave you. And over all these virtues put on love, which binds them all together in perfect unity."

There are items you don't take and there are items you should have with you as you travel through this life for God. How we treat each other is a vital part of the trip. If we are all the same and are all forgiven, then we need to work to help each other. That is why *"compassion, kindness, humility, gentleness and patience"* are to be part of every believers life. These help us *"bear with each other."* In other words we are to work at not provoking each other or getting on each other's nerves. The toughest part of this is remembering we are to *"forgive whatever grievances you may have against one another."* This covers a multitude of sins and circumstances and is only possible when we remember we are forgiving others as Jesus has forgiven us.

What do we take with us? We take the love of Christ and make it part of our life. *"The disciples were called Christians first at Antioch."*[131] They so reflected Jesus Christ and his love that people started calling them 'Christ like.' Paul is saying our love will bring the church and believers together and remove the barriers that often separate them. Love is the glue that holds the church together.

HOW TO ENJOY THE TRIP

"Let the peace of Christ rule in your hearts, since as members of one body you were called to peace. And be thankful. Let the word of Christ dwell in you richly as you teach and admonish one another with all wisdom, and as you sing psalms, hymns and spiritual songs with gratitude in your hearts to God. And whatever you do, whether in word or deed, do it all in the name of the Lord Jesus, giving thanks to God the Father through him."

Why go on a trip and not enjoy it? After getting your sins forgiven and a promise of eternal life why would anyone be sad or mad at God? We are supposed to enjoy our lives as believers. There are items we remove or don't take with us. There are items we need to make the trip better and there are attitudes that make enjoying the trip possible. This starts with the peace of Christ in our hearts. Jesus was clear, *"Peace I leave with you; my peace I give you."*[132] This is not about compromise. Peace to the world is usually a time when people compromise so they can get to a position of strength and defeat the other person or country. Peace brings real peace. No more worrying about God's justice and punishment, instead the person is filled with thankfulness for all Christ has done for them.

The individual must include the Word of Christ in his/her life if he/she is going to discover the joy and happiness that God has prepared for him/her. This is designed to keep the believer on the right track and should he/she stray gives him/her directions how to get back where he/she needs to be.[133]

This new life should lead to a change in spirit that is evident in music. Now, before I continue, I have to confess I cannot sing. That is not an understatement. One night recently my wife was joking with me and asked me to sing her to sleep. So, just to show her what a dangerous thing she had asked for, I started and in moments she was begging me to stop. I really am that bad. Last month the piano tuner was at the church and wanted me to hear what was wrong with the piano before he fixed it. Bad move on his part. He played two notes and said how they were different and flat or sharp and were not supposed to sound like that. They sounded perfectly fine to me. I was wondering why we were getting the thing tuned. That is why I love what Paul said here. He told them to *"sing psalms, hymns and spiritual songs[134] with gratitude in your hearts to God."*[135] People who cannot sing, like me, should not burden others with bad singing. They should at least not be the loudest voice in the room. I said I cannot sing, and I cannot tell two notes beside each other apart but I know what is good music, and what isn't. Music is to bring joy and, for some of us, that means it happens mostly in our hearts. I know all about making a joyful noise to God and I know he can hear what is in my heart.[136]

Everything we do should be done in the name of Jesus. Actions and words are covered equally. The best way to approach this is by asking yourself if this is something you would do if Jesus was with you. Then remember His Holy Spirit is with you.

We should do nothing sinful or that would embarrass God. In all this we need to be thankful to God the Father for all He has done, all He is doing and all He has planned for us.

AS WE TRAVEL...

As we travel toward eternity it is not about what we are against. It is about what we are for.

We are for JESUS.

We are for the KINGDOM of God.

We are for JOYFUL living without fear or guilt.

We are Christian believers, children of God, living our lives for our Lord and Savior, Jesus Christ, the Son of God.

So we should ENJOY THE TRIP!

EPILOGUE

This book is about the elementary teachings of the Christian faith. These will strengthen you as you discover your personal gifts, calling and ministry in the family of God and in your local church. These are the basics and you should know and understand each one. You should expect to use them to go much deeper and learn so much more. My grandson, who is in kindergarten, has a long way to go and a lot more to learn before he gets to his college graduation. After his first day of kindergarten his mother sent out another picture. He is sacked out in bed sleeping. The first day was a lot more than he expected. His mother put a caption on the picture, 'exhausted.' This may seem like you have covered a lot here but in time you will realize this is just the ABC's of the Christian faith. There will be times you may need to go back and cover some of these again but always remember this is the elementary level. You have been learning the 123's of the Christian faith.

Each of us has a lot more to learn and a long way to go before we stand before the throne of God. This is when we will want to hear "*Well done, good and faithful servant! You have been faithful with a few things; I will put you in charge of many things. Come and share your master's happiness!*".[137]

Don't be discouraged and don't ever give up. The trip is worth the destination. I spent many weeks traveling in the back of my parent's station wagon. Yet, it is not the trip I remember most, it is the destinations we went to. You may think the trip is long but I guarantee it will be worth it in the end.

Now, get some sleep, tomorrow is the second day of school and you still have a lot to learn.[138]

Other books and materials available at
bobhighlands.com

Last to Leave
*What the Bible really says
about the end of time.*

The Real Jesus
Journals and Study Guides
Volumes 1-4

The Journey
*The Six basic truths that are
the foundation of the Christian Faith*

Is This Heaven For Real
*A Biblical exposition
of the book 'Heaven is For Real'*

Removing the Mask
*A Monograph On Developing Open
Communications in Local Church Leadership*

The Story Unfolds
*A personal journey through
the Word of God*

END NOTES:

ELEMENTARY CHRISTIANITY

[1] Hebrews 6.1
[2] Hebrews 6.1-2

THE FOUNDATION

[3] http://www.cracked.com/article_20191_6-military-fakes-you-wont-believe-fooled-world.html Accessed February 6, 2014 Is the source for this story.
[4] Ibid
[5] Mark 14.44
[6] 2 Timothy 1.15
[7] http://www.wnd.com/2014/02/poll-hunger-games-harry-potter-are-biblical/ Accessed February 14, 2014
[8] Hebrews 6.1-2 NRSV
[9] 2 Corinthians 12.2 Paul was taken to the third heaven. The first heaven is the sky. The second heaven is prophetic language dealing with position, authority and power. The third heaven is the location of God's throne and our eternal home.
[10] Matthew7:24-27
[11] http://www.cnn.com/2013/06/12/world/asia/worlds-oldest-person-dies/ accessed February 16, 2014
[12] Ibid

LIFE'S DIRECTION

[13] Robert Highlands, *The Journey The six basic truths that are the foundation of the Christian faith* (2010)
[14] Luke 15.11-24
[15] (http://www.ryot.org/16-year-old-rich-kids-defense-for-drinking-driving-and-killing-4-affluenza/497245 accessed February 15, 2014
[16] Matthew 3.4
[17] Matthew 3.5
[18] Matthew 3.2
[19] John 4.17
[20] Acts 2.38
[21] Acts 2.41
[22] Acts 3.19

TRAVELING WITH GOD

[23] 2 Chronicles 18.1-34 tells this story
[24] 2 Chronicles 18.16
[25] 2 Chronicles 18.27
[26] Genesis 30.24 through Genesis 50.26 has the story of Joseph's life
[27] Genesis 50.15
[28] Genesis 50.16-17
[29] Genesis 50.19.21
[30] Acts Chapter 9

[31] 2 Corinthians 11.21-23

[32] 2 Corinthians 11.23

[33] 2 Corinthians 11.23b-27

[34] Romans 8.28

[35] Ethel is her real name but the last name and where she lived is withheld in respect to family members.

LEARNING TO FOLLOW DIRECTIONS

[36] Galatians 5.21

[37] http://www.sodahead.com/united-states/fatal-car-crashes-by-marijuana-smokers-is-up-by-300-over-the-last-decade-will-this-upward-trend-co/question-4204713/?link=ibaf&q=&esrc=s accessed February 28, 2014

[38] Janie B. Cheaney, "Foolish defiance," World Magazine, February 22, 2014 p. 20

[39] Psalm 10.4 NASB

[40] Acts 2.38-39

[41] Romans 6.3-4

[42] 1 Peter 2.21

[43] Acts 2.38

[44] Mark 1.8

[45] Mark 1.8

[46] Acts 11.16

[47] John 15.16 RSV

[48] 2 Timothy 3.12, Mark 10.38b

[49] John 15.20

[50] 2 Timothy 3.12

[51] John 13.14

[52] Janie B. Cheaney, "Foolish defiance," *World Magazine*, February 22, 2014 p. 20

[53] Job 38.4-6

[54] Kenneth E. Jones, "Isaiah," in *The Wesleyan Bible Commentary Volume III*, ed. Charles W. Carter (Grand Rapids: William B. Eerdmans Publishing Company, 1969)

[55] Job 38.11 NIV

YOUR POSITION ON THE TEAM

[56] http://www.mfooz.com/bblog/?p=589 accessed March 6, 2014

[57] 1 Corinthians 12.4-6 NASB

[58] Hebrews 2.4

[59] Colossians 4.17

[60] Romans 8.28

[61] 1 Corinthians 12.27

[62] http://www.baseball-almanac.com/quotes/designated_hitter_quotes.shtml accessed March 6, 2014

[63] http://www.baseball-almanac.com/quotes/designated_hitter_quotes.shtml accessed March 6, 2014

[64] Ephesians 4.11

[65] 1 Corinthians 12.27

[66] Luke 18.15-17

[67] Mark 16.18

[68] Acts 6.6

69 Acts 19.6 NOTE: Six times believers are filled with the Holy Spirit in the book of Acts but only three times is there any reference to the laying on of hands. It can happen this way but it is not the only way.

70 1 Timothy 5.22

71 2 Timothy 1.6

72 1 Corinthians 12.4-6

THE NEXT STEP

73 http://mentalfloss.com/article/20849/quick-8-eight-people-who-have-been-cryonically-preserved-and-one-who-wasn't accessed March 13, 2014

74 http://www.cbsnews.com/news/ted-williams-frozen-in-two-pieces/ accessed March 13, 2014

75 Jesus called it Abraham's bosom. This is another name for heaven.

76 Hebrews 9.27

77 2 Timothy 4.8, 2 Peter 2.9-10

78 1 Corinthians 15.51

79 2 Corinthians 12.2 makes reference to the third heaven and calls it Paradise.

80 Matthew 22.31-32

81 Luke 16.22-23

82 1 Corinthians 15.44

83 1 Corinthians 15.42

84 1 Corinthians 15.43

85 1 Corinthians 15.43

86 1 Corinthians 15.50

87 1 Corinthians 15.50

88 1 Kings 17.17-24

89 II Kings 4.20-37

90 II Kings 13.21

91 Luke 7.11-16

92 Mark 5.35-42

93 John 11.1-44

94 Matthew 27.51.53

95 Acts 9.36-41

96 Acts 20.7-12

97 1 Corinthians 15.51

98 Burpo, Todd with Vincent, Lynn. *Heaven is for Real*. Nashville: Thomas Nelson, 2010

99 Bob Highlands III, *Is This Heaven for Real*, USA: 2012

100 Matthew 25.46

101 1 Corinthians 15.51-52

ONE FINAL APPOINTMENT

102 Luke 19.10

103 Hebrews 9.27

104 Mathew 25.44

105 Luke 19.9

106 Luke 15.3-7

107 Luke 15.8-10

108 Luke 15.11-32

109 Hebrews 9.28

[110] Romans 5.8

[111] Romans 3.23

[112] Ephesians 1.7

[113] Romans 6.23

[114] John 14.6

[115] 1 Corinthians 15.50-54

[116] en.wikipedia.org/wiki/World_population Accessed March 28, 2014

[117] http://www.english-online.at/geography/world-population/world-population-growth.htm accessed March 28, 2014

[118] 2 Corinthians 5.10

[119] Matthew 25.44

[120] Matthew 25.44

[121] 1Corinthians 6.9-10, Galatians 5.19-21, Ephesians 5.5, Revelation 21.8

[122] Revelation 21.27

[123] John 14.6

ROAD TRIP WITH GOD

[124] This is long before seat belts and well before there were car seats for kids of certain weights.

[125] Colossians 3.1-4

[126] Colossians 3.5-8

[127] Colossians 3.9-11

[128] Philippians 3.5

[129] Philippians 3.5

[130] Galatians 3.28

[131] Acts 11.26

[132] John 14.27

[133] 2 Timothy 3.16-17 shows the four ways scripture is designed to help the believer stay or get back on track.

[134] Psalms deals with striking or the use of instruments. Hymns is about the words that form thanks and praise and putting them together is how we get spiritual songs.

[135] Ephesians 5.19

[136] This is a personal pet peeve with me. Why is it some really bad singers think they should be allowed to sing in front of the church and it is somehow uplifting. If it is not their gift from God they should not burden others with it or the lack of it.

EPILOGUE

[137] Matthew 25.21, 23 NIV

[138] To go deeper on these basic you can get more scripture references and background in the book *"The Journey – The six truths that are the foundation of the Christian faith"* by Bob Highlands III © 2010